Modern Critical Interpretations

Thomas Hardy's
Tess of the D'Urbervilles

Modern Critical Interpretations

The Oresteia
Beowulf
The General Prologue to
   The Canterbury Tales
The Pardoner's Tale
The Knight's Tale
The Divine Comedy
Exodus
Genesis
The Gospels
The Iliad
The Book of Job
Volpone
Doctor Faustus
The Revelation of St.
   John the Divine
The Song of Songs
Oedipus Rex
The Aeneid
The Duchess of Malfi
Antony and Cleopatra
As You Like It
Coriolanus
Hamlet
Henry IV, Part I
Henry IV, Part II
Henry V
Julius Caesar
King Lear
Macbeth
Measure for Measure
The Merchant of Venice
A Midsummer Night's
   Dream
Much Ado About
   Nothing
Othello
Richard II
Richard III
The Sonnets
Taming of the Shrew
The Tempest
Twelfth Night
The Winter's Tale
Emma
Mansfield Park
Pride and Prejudice
The Life of Samuel
   Johnson
Moll Flanders
Robinson Crusoe
Tom Jones
The Beggar's Opera
Gray's Elegy
Paradise Lost
The Rape of the Lock
Tristram Shandy
Gulliver's Travels

Evelina
The Marriage of Heaven
   and Hell
Songs of Innocence and
   Experience
Jane Eyre
Wuthering Heights
Don Juan
The Rime of the Ancient
   Mariner
Bleak House
David Copperfield
Hard Times
A Tale of Two Cities
Middlemarch
The Mill on the Floss
Jude the Obscure
The Mayor of
   Casterbridge
The Return of the Native
Tess of the D'Urbervilles
The Ode of Keats
Frankenstein
Vanity Fair
Barchester Towers
The Prelude
The Red Badge of
   Courage
The Scarlet Letter
The Ambassadors
Daisy Miller, The Turn
   of the Screw, and
   Other Tales
The Portrait of a Lady
Billy Budd, Benito Cer-
   eno, Bartleby the Scriv-
   ener, and Other Tales
Moby-Dick
The Tales of Poe
Walden
Adventures of
   Huckleberry Finn
The Life of Frederick
   Douglass
Heart of Darkness
Lord Jim
Nostromo
A Passage to India
Dubliners
A Portrait of the Artist as
   a Young Man
Ulysses
Kim
The Rainbow
Sons and Lovers
Women in Love
1984
Major Barbara

Man and Superman
Pygmalion
St. Joan
The Playboy of the
   Western World
The Importance of Being
   Earnest
Mrs. Dalloway
To the Lighthouse
My Antonia
An American Tragedy
Murder in the Cathedral
The Waste Land
Absalom, Absalom!
Light in August
Sanctuary
The Sound and the Fury
The Great Gatsby
A Farewell to Arms
The Sun Also Rises
Arrowsmith
Lolita
The Iceman Cometh
Long Day's Journey Into
   Night
The Grapes of Wrath
Miss Lonelyhearts
The Glass Menagerie
A Streetcar Named
   Desire
Their Eyes Were
   Watching God
Native Son
Waiting for Godot
Herzog
All My Sons
Death of a Salesman
Gravity's Rainbow
All the King's Men
The Left Hand of
   Darkness
The Brothers Karamazov
Crime and Punishment
Madame Bovary
The Interpretation of
   Dreams
The Castle
The Metamorphosis
The Trial
Man's Fate
The Magic Mountain
Montaigne's Essays
Remembrance of Things
   Past
The Red and the Black
Anna Karenina
War and Peace

These and other titles in preparation

Modern Critical Interpretations

Thomas Hardy's
Tess of the D'Urbervilles

Edited and with an introduction by
Harold Bloom
Sterling Professor of the Humanities
Yale University

Chelsea House Publishers
NEW YORK ◊ PHILADELPHIA

Copyright © 1987 by Chelsea House Publishers,
a division of Main Line Book Co.

3 5 7 9 8 6 4

Introduction © 1987 by Harold Bloom

Printed and bound in the United States of America

∞ The paper used in this publication meets the
minimum requirements of the American National
Standard for Permanence of Paper for Printed Library
Materials, Z39.48–1984.

Library of Congress Cataloging-in-Publication Data

Thomas Hardy's Tess of the d'Urbervilles.

   (Modern critical interpretations)
   Bibliography: p.
   Includes index.
   1. Hardy, Thomas, 1840–1928. Tess of the
d'Urbervilles.   I. Bloom, Harold.   II. Series.
PR4748.T46   1986   823'.8   86–14762
ISBN 0–87754–744–0

Contents

Editor's Note / vii

Introduction / 1
   HAROLD BLOOM

Colour and Movement in Hardy's *Tess
of the D'Urbervilles* / 9
   TONY TANNER

"The Perfection of Species" and Hardy's Tess / 25
   BRUCE JOHNSON

Tess: The Making of a Pure Woman / 45
   MARY JACOBUS

Tess of the D'Urbervilles: Repetition as Immanent
Design / 61
   J. HILLIS MILLER

Pure Tess: Hardy on Knowing a Woman / 87
   KATHLEEN BLAKE

Hardy: "Full-Hearted Evensong" / 103
   PHILIP M. WEINSTEIN

Chronology / 119

Contributors / 123

Bibliography / 125

Acknowledgments / 129

Index / 130

Editor's Note

This book gathers together a representative selection of the best criticism available upon Thomas Hardy's novel *Tess of the D'Urbervilles*, reprinted here in the chronological order of its original publication. I am grateful to Jennifer Wagner for her industry and judgment in helping to research this volume.

The editor's introduction relates Hardy to his precursors Schopenhauer and Shelley, while defining the author's irony in *Tess* as biblical in its style, though scarcely in its substance. Tony Tanner begins the chronological sequence of criticism with a sensitive description of the configurations of darkness, color, and movement in *Tess*, as well as elsewhere in Hardy. A Darwinian context for the novel is persuasively suggested by Bruce Johnson, while Mary Jacobus brilliantly argues that Hardy gives us Tess as "not a woman to be admired for her purity or condemned for the lack of it; simply, she is a human being whose right to be is affirmed on every page."

J. Hillis Miller, our leading critic of Hardy, deconstructs *Tess* as a sequence of interpretive repetitions, a reading that my introduction seeks to refute. In a discussion that compares usefully to that of Mary Jacobus, Kathleen Blake sees Hardy as moving in *Tess* towards the "feminism" of *Jude the Obscure*, while portraying Tess both as object of desire and aesthetic object. In the concluding essay, Philip Weinstein argues against Lionel Johnson's judgment (also cited in the editor's introduction) by insisting that "*Tess* is a novel not of failed transcendence but of tragically achieved immersion," and so an evensong about "the release, despoliation, and exhaustion of human resource."

Introduction

For Arthur Schopenhauer, the Will to Live was the true thing-in-itself, not an interpretation but a rapacious, active, universal, and ultimately indifferent drive or desire. Schopenhauer's great work, *The World as Will and Representation*, had the same relation to and influence upon many of the principal nineteenth- and early twentieth-century novelists that Freud's writings have in regard to many of this century's later, crucial masters of prose fiction. Zola, Maupassant, Turgenev, and Tolstoy join Thomas Hardy as Schopenhauer's nineteenth-century heirs, in a tradition that goes on through Proust, Conrad, and Thomas Mann to culminate in aspects of Borges and Beckett, the two most eminent living writers of narrative. Since Schopenhauer (despite Freud's denials) was one of Freud's prime precursors, one could argue that aspects of Freud's influence upon writers simply carry on from Schopenhauer's previous effect. Manifestly, the relation of Schopenhauer to Hardy is different in both kind and degree from the larger sense in which Schopenhauer was Freud's forerunner or Wittgenstein's. A poet-novelist like Hardy turns to a rhetorical speculator like Schopenhauer only because he finds something in his own temperament and sensibility confirmed and strengthened, and not at all as Lucretius turned to Epicurus, or as Whitman was inspired by Emerson.

The true precursor for Hardy was Shelley, whose visionary skepticism permeates the novels as well as the poems and *The Dynasts*. There is some technical debt to George Eliot in the early novels, but Hardy in his depths was little more moved by her than by Wilkie Collins, from whom he also learned elements of craft. Shelley's tragic sense of eros is pervasive throughout Hardy, and ultimately determines Hardy's understanding of his strongest heroines: Bathsheba Everdene, Eustacia Vye, Marty South, Tess Durbeyfield, Sue Bridehead. Between desire and fulfillment in Shelley falls the shadow of the selfhood, a shadow that makes love and what might be called the means of love quite irreconcilable. What M. D. Zabel named as "the aesthetic of incongruity" in Hardy and ascribed to temperamental causes is in a profound way the result of attempting to transmute the procedures of *The Revolt of Islam* and *Epipsychidion* into the supposedly naturalistic novel.

J. Hillis Miller, when he worked more in the mode of a critic of consciousness like Georges Poulet than in the deconstruction of Paul de Man and Jacques Derrida, saw the fate of love in Hardy as being darkened always by a shadow cast by the lover's consciousness itself. Hugh Kenner, with a distaste for Hardy akin to (and perhaps derived from) T. S. Eliot's in *After Strange Gods*, suggested that Miller had created a kind of Proustian Hardy, who turns out to be a case rather than an artist. Hardy was certainly not an artist comparable to Henry James (who dismissed him as a mere imitator of George Eliot) or James Joyce, but the High Modernist shibboleths for testing the novel have now waned considerably, except for a few surviving high priests of Modernism like Kenner. A better guide to Hardy's permanent strength as a novelist was his heir D. H. Lawrence, whose *Rainbow* and *Women in Love* marvelously brought Hardy's legacy to an apotheosis. Lawrence, praising Hardy with a rebel son's ambivalence, associated him with Tolstoy as a tragic writer:

> And this is the quality Hardy shares with the great writers, Shakespeare or Sophocles or Tolstoi, this setting behind the small action of his protagonists the terrific action of unfathomed nature; setting a smaller system of morality, the one grasped and formulated by the human consciousness within the vast, uncomprehended and incomprehensible morality of nature or of life itself, surpassing human consciousness. The difference is, that whereas in Shakespeare or Sophocles the greater, un-comprehended morality, or fate, is actively transgressed and gives active punishment, in Hardy and Tolstoi the lesser, hu-man morality, the mechanical system is actively transgressed, and holds, and punishes the protagonist, whilst the greater morality is only passively, negatively transgressed, it is repre-sented merely as being present in background, in scenery, not taking any active part, having no direct connexion with the pro-tagonist. Œdipus, Hamlet, Macbeth set themselves up against, or find themselves set up against, the unfathomed moral forces of nature, and out of this unfathomed force comes their death. Whereas Anna Karenina, Eustacia, Tess, Sue, and Jude find

themselves up against the established system of human government and morality, they cannot detach themselves, and are brought down. Their real tragedy is that they are unfaithful to the greater unwritten morality, which would have bidden Anna Karenina be patient and wait until she, by virtue of greater right, could take what she needed from society; would have bidden Vronsky detach himself from the system, become an individual, creating a new colony of morality with Anna; would have bidden Eustacia fight Clym for his own soul, and Tess take and claim her Angel, since she had the greater light; would have bidden Jude and Sue endure for very honour's sake, since one must bide by the best that one has known, and not succumb to the lesser good.

("Study of Thomas Hardy")

This seems to me powerful and just, because it catches what is most surprising and enduring in Hardy's novels—the sublime stature and aesthetic dignity of his crucial protagonists—while exposing also his great limitation, his denial of freedom to his best personages. Lawrence's prescription for what would have saved Eustacia and Clym, Tess and Angel, Sue and Jude, is perhaps not as persuasive. He speaks of them as though they were Gudrun and Gerald, and thus have failed to be Ursula and Birkin. It is Hardy's genius that they are what they had to be: as imperfect as their creator and his vision, as impure as his language and his plotting, and finally painful and memorable to us:

> Note that, in this bitterness, delight,
> Since the imperfect is so hot in us,
> Lies in flawed words and stubborn sounds.

II

Of all the novels of Hardy, *Tess of the D'Urbervilles* now appeals to the widest audience. The book's popularity with the common reader has displaced the earlier ascendancy of *The Return of the Native*. It can even be asserted that Hardy's novel has proved to be prophetic of a sensibility by no means fully emergent in 1891. Nearly a century later, the book sometimes seems to have moments of vision that are contemporary with us. These tend to come from Hardy's intimate sympathy with his heroine, a sympathy that verges upon paternal love. It is curious that Hardy is more involved with Tess than with Jude Fawley in *Jude the Obscure*, even though

Jude is closer to being Hardy's surrogate than any other male figure in the novels.

J. Hillis Miller, in the most advanced critical study yet attempted of *Tess*, reads it as "a story about repetition," but by "repetition" Miller appears to mean a linked chain of interpretations. A compulsion to interpret may be the reader's share, and may be Hardy's own stance towards his own novel (and perhaps even extends to Angel Clare's role in the book), but seems to me fairly irrelevant to Tess herself. Since the novel is a story about Tess, I cannot regard it as being "about" repetition, or even one that concerns a difference in repetitions. Hardy's more profound ironies are neither classical nor Romantic, but Biblical, as Miller himself discerns. Classical irony turns upon contrasts between what is said and what is meant, while Romantic irony inhabits the gap between expectation and fulfillment. But Biblical irony appears whenever giant incongruities clash, which happens when Yahweh, who is incommensurate, is closely juxtaposed to men and women and their vain imaginings. When Yahweh devours roast calf under the terebinths at Mamre, or when Jacob wrestles with a nameless one among the Elohim at Penuel, then we are confronted by an irony neither classical nor Romantic.

Hardy, like his master Shelley, is an unbeliever who remains within the literary context of the Bible, and again like Shelley he derives his mode of prophetic irony from the Bible. A striking instance (noted by Hillis Miller) comes in chapter 11:

> In the meantime Alec d'Urberville had pushed on up the slope to clear his genuine doubt as to the quarter of The Chase they were in. He had, in fact, ridden quite at random for over an hour, taking any turning that came to hand in order to prolong companionship with her, and giving far more attention to Tess's moonlit person than to any wayside object. A little rest for the jaded animal being desirable, he did not hasten his search for landmarks. A clamber over the hill into the adjoining vale brought him to the fence of a highway whose contours he recognized, which settled the question of their whereabouts. D'Urberville thereupon turned back; but by this time the moon had quite gone down, and partly on account of the fog The Chase was wrapped in thick darkness, although morning was not far off. He was obliged to advance with outstretched hands to avoid contact with the boughs, and discovered that to hit the exact spot from which he had started was at first entirely be-

yond him. Roaming up and down, round and round, he at length heard a slight movement of the horse close at hand; and the sleeve of his overcoat unexpectedly caught his foot.

"Tess!" said d'Urberville.

There was no answer. The obscurity was now so great that he could see absolutely nothing but a pale nebulousness at his feet, which represented the white muslin figure he had left upon the dead leaves. Everything else was blackness alike. D'Urberville stooped; and heard a gentle regular breathing. He knelt and bent lower, till her breath warmed his face, and in a moment his cheek was in contact with hers. She was sleeping soundly, and upon her eyelashes there lingered tears.

Darkness and silence ruled everywhere around. Above them rose the primeval yews and oaks of The Chase, in which were poised gentle roosting birds in their last nap; and about them stole the hopping rabbits and hares. But, might some say, where was Tess's guardian angel? where was the providence of her simple faith? Perhaps, like that other god of whom the ironical Tishbite spoke, he was talking, or he was pursuing, or he was in a journey, or he was sleeping and not to be awaked.

Why it was that upon this beautiful feminine tissue, sensitive as gossamer, and practically blank as snow as yet, there should have been traced such a coarse pattern as it was doomed to receive; why so often the coarse appropriates the finer thus, the wrong man the woman, the wrong woman the man, many thousand years of analytical philosophy have failed to explain to our sense of order. One may, indeed, admit the possibility of a retribution lurking in the present catastrophe. Doubtless some of Tess d'Urberville's mailed ancestors rollicking home from a fray had dealt the same measure even more ruthlessly towards peasant girls of their time. But though to visit the sins of the fathers upon the children may be a morality good enough for divinities, it is scorned by average human nature; and it there-fore does not mend the matter.

As Tess's own people down in those retreats are never tired of saying among each other in their fatalistic way: "It was to be." There lay the pity of it. An immeasurable social chasm was to divide our heroine's personality thereafter from that previous self of hers who stepped from her mother's door to try her fortune at Trantridge poultry-farm.

The ironical Tishbite is the savage Elijah the prophet, who mocks the priests of Baal, urging them: "Cry aloud: for he is a god; either he is talking, or he is pursuing, or he is in a journey, or peradventure he sleepeth, and must be awaked." Elijah's irony depends upon the incommensurateness of Yahweh and the human—all too human—Baal. Hardy's irony cannot be what Hillis Miller deconstructively wishes it to be when he rather remarkably suggests that Tess herself is "like the prophets of Baal," nor does it seem right to call Yahweh's declaration that He is a jealous (or zealous) God "the divine lust for vengeance," as Miller does. Yahweh, after all, has just given the Second Commandment against making graven images or idols, such as the Baal whom Elijah mocks. Hardy associates Alec's "violation" of Tess with a destruction of pastoral innocence, which he scarcely sees as Baal-worship or idolatry. His emphasis is precisely that no mode of religion, revealed or natural, could defend Tess from an over-determined system in which the only thing-in-itself is the rapacious Will to Live, a Will that itself is, as it were, the curse of Yahweh upon the hungry generations.

Repetition in *Tess* is repetition as Schopenhauer saw it, which is little different from how Hardy and Freud subsequently saw it. What is re-peated, compulsively, is a unitary desire that is rapacious, indifferent, and universal. The pleasures of repetition in Hardy's *Tess* are not interpre-tive and perspectival, and so engendered by difference, but are actually masochistic, in the erotogenic sense, and so ensue from the necessity of similarity. Hardy's pragmatic version of the aesthetic vision in this novel is essentially sado-masochistic, and the sufferings of poor Tess give an equivocal pleasure of repetition to the reader. The book's extraordinary popularity partly results from its exquisitely subtle and deeply sympathetic unfolding of the torments of Tess, a pure woman because a pure nature, and doomed to suffer merely because she is so much a natural woman. The poet Lionel Johnson, whose early book (1895) on Hardy still seems to me unsurpassed, brought to the reading of *Tess* a spirit that was antithetically both Shelleyan and Roman Catholic:

> as a girl of generous thought and sentiment, rich in beauty, rich in the natural joys of life, she is brought into collision with the harshness of life. . . . The world was very strong; her conscience was blinded and bewildered; she did some things nobly, and some despairingly: but there is nothing, not even in studies of criminal anthropology or of morbid pathology, to suggest that she was wholly an irresponsible victim of her own tempera-

ment, and of adverse circumstances. . . . She went through fire
and water, and made no true use of them: she is pitiable, but
not admirable.

Johnson is very clear-sighted, but perhaps too much the Catholic
moralist. To the common reader, Tess is both pitiable and admirable, as
Hardy wanted her to be. Is it admirable, though, that, by identifying with
her, the reader takes a masochistic pleasure in her suffering? Aesthetically,
I would reply yes, but the question remains a disturbing one. When the
black flag goes slowly up the staff and we know that the beautiful Tess has
been executed, do we reside in Hardy's final ironies, or do we experience a
pleasure of repetition that leaves us void of interpretive zeal, yet replete
with the gratification of a drive beyond the pleasure principle?

Colour and Movement in Hardy's *Tess of the D'Urbervilles*

Tony Tanner

I have suggested [earlier] that the destiny of Tess comes to us as a cumulation of visible omens. It is also a convergence of omens and to explain what I mean I want to add a few comments on the part played in her life by the sun, altars and tombs, and finally walking and travelling. When we first see Tess with the other dancing girls we read that they are all bathed in sunshine. Hardy, ever conscious of effects of light, describes how their hair reflects various colours in the sunlight. More, "as each and all of them were warmed without by the sun, so each of them had a private little sun for her soul to bask in." They are creatures of the sun, warmed and nourished by the source of all heat and life. Tess starts sun-blessed. At the dairy, the sun is at its most active as a cause of the fertile surgings which animate all nature. "Rays from the sunrise drew forth the buds and stretched them into stalks, lifted up sap in noiseless streams, opened petals, and sucked out scents in invisible jets and breathings." This is the profoundly sensuous atmosphere in which Tess, despite mental hesitations, blooms into full female ripeness. Hardy does something very suggestive here in his treatment of the times of day. Tess and Angel rise very early, before the sun. They seem to themselves "the first persons up of all the world." The light is still "half-compounded, aqueous," as though the business of creating animated forms has not yet begun. They are compared to Adam and Eve. As so often when Tess is getting involved with the superior power of a man, the atmosphere is misty, but this time it is cold mist, the sunless fogs which precede the dawn. In this particular light of a cool watery whiteness, Tess

From *Critical Quarterly* 10, no. 3 (Autumn 1968). © 1968 by Tony Tanner.

appears to Angel as "a visionary essence of woman," something ghostly, "merely a soul at large." He calls her, among other things, Artemis (who lived, of course, in perpetual celibacy). In this sunless light Tess appears to Angel as unsexed, sexless, the sort of non-physical spiritualised essence he, in his impotent spirituality, wants. (At the end he marries "a spiritualized image of Tess"). But Tess is inescapably flesh and blood. And when the sun does come up, she reverts from divine essence to physical milkmaid: "her teeth, lips and eyes scintillated in the sunbeams, and she was again the dazzlingly fair dairymaid only . . . . " (That placing of "only" is typical of the strength of Hardy's prose.) Soon after this, the dairyman tells his story of the seduction of a young girl; "none of them but herself seemed to see the sorrow of it." And immediately we read, "the evening sun was now ugly to her, like a great inflamed wound in the sky." Sex is a natural instinct which however can lead to lives of utter misery. The same sun that blesses, can curse.

Tess drifts into marriage with Angel (her most characteristic way of moving in a landscape is a "quiescent glide"), because "every wave of her blood . . . was a voice that joined with nature in revolt against her scrupulousness," but meanwhile "at half-past six the sun settled down upon the levels, with the aspect of a great forge in the heavens." This suggests not a drawing-up into growth, but a slow inexorable downward crushing force, through an image linked to that machinery which will later pummel her body. It is as though the universe turns metallic against Tess, just as we read when Angel rejects her that there is in him a hard negating force "like a vein of metal in a soft loam." This is the metal which her soft flesh runs up against. Other omens follow on her journey towards her wedding. Her feeling that she has seen the d'Urberville coach before; the postillion who takes them to church and who has "a permanent running wound on the outside of his right leg"; the ominous "afternoon crow" and so on. I want to point to another omen, when the sun seems to single out Tess in a sinister way. It is worth reminding ourselves that when Angel finally does propose to Tess she is quite sun-drenched. They are standing on the "red-brick" floor and the sun slants in "upon her inclining face, upon the blue veins of her temple, upon her naked arm, and her neck, and into the depths of her hair." Now, on what should be the first night of her honeymoon we read: "The sun was so low on that short, last afternoon of the year that it shone in through a small opening and formed a golden staff which stretched across to her skirt, where it made a spot like a paint-mark set upon her." She has been marked before—first, with the blood of a dying beast, now with a mark from the setting sun. We find other descriptions of how the sun shines on Tess subsequently, but let us return to that crimson bed which, I suggested, effectively marked the end of Tess's journey. "A shaft of dazzling sunlight glanced into the room, revealing heavy, old-fashioned furniture, crimson damask hangings, and an enormous four-poster bedstead." The sun and the redness which have marked Tess's life, now converge at the moment of her approaching death. Finally Tess takes her last rest on the altar of Stonehenge. She speaks to Angel— again, it is before dawn, that sunless part of the day when he can communicate with her.

> "Did they sacrifice to God here?" asked she.
> "No," said he.
> "Who to?"
> "I believe to the sun. That lofty stone set away by itself is in
> the direction of the sun, which will presently rise behind it."

When the sun does rise it also reveals the policemen closing in, for it is society which demands a specific revenge upon Tess. But in the configuration of omens which, I think, is the major part of the book, Tess is indeed a victim, sacrificed to the sun. The heathen temple is fitting, since of course Tess is descended from Pagan d'Urberville, and Hardy makes no scruple about asserting that women "retain in their souls far more of the Pagan fantasy of their remote forefathers than of the systematized religion taught their race at a later date." This raises an important point. Is Tess a victim of society, or of nature? Who wants her blood, who is after her, the policemen, or the sun? Or are they in some sadistic conspiracy so that we see nature and society converging on Tess to destroy her? I will return to this question.

To the convergence of redness and the sun we must add the great final fact of the altar, an altar which Tess approaches almost gratefully, and on which she takes up her sacrificial position with exhausted relief. She says (I have run some of her words to Angel together): "I don't want to go any further, Angel. . . . Can't we bide here? . . . you used to say at Talbothays that I was a heathen. So now I am at home . . . I like very much to be here." Fully to be human is partly to be heathen, as the figure of Tess on the altar makes clear. (And after all what did heathen originally mean? —someone who lived on the heath; and what was a pagan?—someone who lived in a remote village. The terms only acquire their opprobrium after the advent of Christianity. Similarly Hardy points out that Sunday was originally the sun's day—a spiritual superstructure has been imposed on a physical source.) Tess's willingness to take her place on the stone of death has been manifested before. After she returns from the rape we read "her depression was then terrible, and she could have hidden herself in a tomb." On her marriage night, Angel sleepwalks into her room, saying "Dead! Dead! Dead!. . . My wife—dead, dead!" He picks her up, kisses her (which he can now only manage when he is unconscious), and carries her over a racing river. Tess almost wants to jog him so that they can fall to their deaths: but Angel can negotiate the dangers of turbulent water just as he can suppress all passion. His steps are not directed towards the movement of the waters but to the stillness of stone. He takes Tess and lays her in an "empty stone coffin" in the "ruined choir." In Angel's life of suppressed spontaneity and the negation of passional feeling, this is the most significant thing that he does. He encoffins the sexual instinct, then lies down beside Tess. The deepest inclinations of his psyche, his very being, have been revealed.

Later on, when things are utterly desperate for Tess's family and they literally have no roof over their heads, they take refuge by the church in which the family vaults are kept (where "the bones of her ancestors—her useless ancestors—lay entombed.") In their exhaustion they erect an old "four-post bedstead" over the vaults. We see again the intimate proximity of the bed and the grave. This sombre contiguity also adumbrates the ambiguous relief which Tess later finds in her crimson four-post-bed which is also very close to death. On this occasion Tess enters the church and pauses by the "tombs of the family" and "the door of her ancestral sepulchre." It is at this point that one of the tomb effigies moves, and Alec plays his insane jest on her by appearing to leap from a tomb. Again, we are invited to make the starkest sort of comparison without any exegesis from Hardy. Angel, asleep, took Tess in his arms and laid her in a coffin. Alec, however, seems to wake up from the tomb, a crude but animated threat to Tess in her quest for peace. Angel's instinct towards stillness is countered by Alec's instinct for sexual motion. Together they add up to a continuous process in which Tess is simply caught up. For it is both men who drive Tess to her death: Angel by his spiritualised rejection, Alec by his sexual attacks. It is notable that both these men are also cut off from any fixed community; they have both broken away from traditional attitudes and dwellings. Angel roams in his thought; Alec roams in his lust. They are both drifters of the sort who have an unsettling, often destructive impact in the Hardy world. Tess is a pure product of nature; but she is nature subject to complex and contradictory pressures. Angel wants her spiritual image without her body (when he finds out about her sexual past he simply denies her identity "the woman I have been loving is not you"); Alec wants only her body and is indifferent to anything we might call her soul, her distinctly human inwardness. The effect of this opposed wrenching on her wholeness is to induce a sort of inner rift which develops into something we would now call schizophrenia. While still at Talbothays she says one day: "I do know that our souls can be made to go outside our bodies when we are alive." Her method is to fix the mind on a remote star and "you will soon find that you are hundreds and hundreds o' miles away from your body, which you don't seem to want at all." The deep mystery by which consciousness can seek to be delivered from the body which sustains it, is one which Hardy had clearly before him. That an organism can be generated which then wishes to repudiate the very grounds of its existence obviously struck Hardy as providing a very awesome comment on the nature of nature. Tess is robbed of her integrated singleness, divided by two men, two forces. (This gives extra point to the various crosses she passes on her travels; the cross not only indicating torture, but that opposition between the vertical and the horizontal which, as I shall try to show, is ultimately the source of Tess's—and man's—sufferings in Hardy.) It is no wonder that when Alec worries and pursues her at the very door of her ancestor's vault, she should bend down and whisper that line of terrible simplicity—"Why am I on the wrong side of this door?" (A relevant poem of great power is "A Wasted Illness" of which I quote three stanzas which are very apt for Tess:

> "Where lies the end
> To this foul way?" I asked with weakening breath.
> Thereon ahead I saw a door extend—
> The door to Death.
>
> It loomed more clear:
> "At last!" I cried. "The all-delivering door!"
> And then, I know not how, it grew less near
> Than theretofore.
>
> And back slid I
> Along the galleries by which I came,
> And tediously the day returned, and sky,
> And life—the same.)

Tess at this moment is utterly unplaced, with no refuge and no comfort. She can only stumble along more and rougher roads; increasingly vulnerable, weary and helpless, increasingly remote from her body. Her only solution is to break through that "all-delivering door," the door from life to death which opens on the only home left to her. This she does, by stabbing Alec and then taking her place on the ritual altar. She has finally spilled all the blood that tormented her; she can then abandon the torments of animateness and seek out the lasting repose she has earned.

This brings me to what is perhaps the most searching of all Hardy's preoccupations—walking, travelling, movement of all kinds. Somewhere at the heart of his vision is a profound sense of what we may call the mystery of motion. *Tess of the D'Urbervilles* opens with a man staggering on rickety legs down a road, and it is his daughter we shall see walking throughout the book. Phase the Second opens, once again, simply with an unexplained scene of laboured walking. "The basket was heavy and the bundle was large, but she lugged them along like a person who did not find her especial burden in material things. Occasionally she stopped to rest in a mechanical way by some gate or post; and then, giving the baggage another hitch upon her full round arm, went steadily on again." Such visualized passages carry the meaning of the novel, even down to the material burdens which weigh down that plump, vulnerable flesh: the meaning is both mute and unmistakable. At the start of Phase the Third, again Tess moves: "she left her home for the second time." At first the journey seems easy and comfortable in "a hired trap"; but soon she gets out and walks, and her journey again leads her into portents of the life ahead of her. "The journey over the intervening uplands and lowlands of Egdon, when she reached them, was a more troublesome walk than she had antici- pated, the distance being actually but a few miles. It was two hours, owing to sundry turnings, 'ere she found herself on a summit commanding the long-sought-for vale." The road to the peaceful vale of death is longer and harder than she thinks. Always Tess has to move, usually to harsher and more punishing territories, and always Hardy makes sure we *see* her. After Angel has banished her: "instead of a bride with boxes and trunks which others bore, we see her a lonely woman with a basket and a bundle in her own porterage." Later she walks to Emminster Vicarage on her abortive journey to see Angel's parents. She starts off briskly but by the end she is weary, and there are omens by the way. For instance, from one eminence she looks down at endless little fields, "so numerous that they look from this height like the meshes of a net." And again she passes a stone cross, Cross-in-Hand, which stands "desolate and silent, to mark the site of a miracle, or murder, or both." (Note the hint of the profound ambivalence and ambiguity of deeds and events.) At the end of this journey there is nobody at home and there follows the incident of Tess losing her walking boots, another physical reminder that the walking gets harder and harder for her. "Her journey back was rather a meander than a march. It had no sprightliness, no purpose; only a tendency." Her movements do get more leaden throughout, and by the end Hardy confronts us with one of the strangest phenomena of existence — motion without volition. (Interestingly enough, Conrad approaches the same phenomenon in *The Secret Agent* where walking is also the most insistent motif.) The only relief in her walking is that as it gets harder it also approaches nearer to darkness. Thus when she is summoned back to her family: "She plunged into the chilly equinoctial darkness . . . for her fifteen miles' walk under the steely stars"; and later during this walk from another eminence she "looked from that height into the abyss of chaotic shade which was all that revealed itself of the vale on whose further side she was born." She is indeed returning home, just as Oedipus was returning home on all his journeyings. Perhaps the ultimate reduction of Tess, the distillation of her fate, is to be seen when she runs after Angel having murdered Alec. Angel turns round. "The tape-like surface of the road diminished in his rear as far as he could see, and as he gazed a moving spot intruded on the white vacuity of its perspective." This scene has been anticipated when Tess was working at Flintcomb-Ash: "the whole field was in colour a desolate drab; it was a complexion without features, as if a face, from chin to brow, should be only an expanse of skin. The sky wore, in another colour, the same likeness; a white vacuity of countenance with the lineaments gone. So these two upper and nether visages confronted each other all day long . . . without anything standing between them but the two girls crawling over the surface of the former like flies." In both cases we see Tess as a moving spot on a white vacuity. And this extreme pictorial reduction seems to me to be right at the heart of Hardy's vision.

To explain what I mean I want to interpose a few comments on some remarkable passages from the earlier novel, *The Return of the Native*. Chapter 1 describes the vast inert heath. Chapter 2 opens "Along the road walked an old man." He in turn sees a tiny speck of movement—"the single atom of life that the scene contained." And this spot is a "lurid red." It is, of course, the reddleman, but I want to emphasise the composition of the scene — the great stillness and the tiny spot of red movement which is the human presence on the heath. Shortly after, the reddleman is scanning the heath (Hardy's world is full of watching eyes) and it is then that he first sees Eustacia Vye. But how he first sees her is described in a passage which seems to me so central to Hardy that I want to quote at length.

> There the form stood, motionless as the hill beneath. Above the plain rose the hill, above the hill rose the barrow, and above the barrow rose the figure. Above the figure there was nothing that could be mapped elsewhere than on a celestial globe.
>
> Such a perfect, delicate, and necessary finish did the figure give to the dark pile of hills that it seemed to be the only obvious justification of their outline. Without it, there was the dome without the lantern; with it the architectural demands of the mass were satisfied. The scene was strangely homogenous. The vale, the upland, the barrow, and the figure above it amounted to unity. Looking at this or that member of the group was not observing a complete thing, but a fraction of a thing.
>
> The form was so much like an organic part of the entire motionless structure that to see it move would have impressed the mind as a strange phenomenon. Immobility being the chief characteristic of that whole which the person formed portion of, the discontinuance of immobility in any quarter suggested confusion.
>
> Yet this is what happened. The figure perceptibly gave up its fixity, shifted a step or two, and turned round.

Here in powerful visual terms is a complete statement about existence. Without the human presence, sheer land and sky seem to have no formal, architectural significance. The human form brings significant outline to the brown mass of earth, the white vacuity of sky. But this moment of satisfying formal harmony depends on stillness, and to be human is to be animated, is to move. Hardy's novels are about "the discontinuance of immobility"; all the confusions that make up his plots are the result of people who perceptibly give up their fixity. To say that this is the very condition of life itself is only to point to the elemental nature of Hardy's art. All plants and all animals move, but much more within the rhythms ordained by their native terrain than humans—who build things like the *Titanic* and go plunging off into the night sea, or who set out in a horse and cart in the middle of the night to reach a distant market, in both cases meeting with disastrous accidents. Only what moves can crash. Eustacia moves on the still heath, breaking up the unity: there is confusion ahead for her. Not indeed that the heath is in a state of absolute fixity; that would imply a dead planet: "the quality of repose appertaining to the scene . . .

was not the repose of actual stagnation, but the apparent repose of incredible slowness." Hardy often reminds us of the mindless insect life
going on near the feet of his bewildered human protagonists; but to the
human eye, which after all determines the felt meaning of the perceptible
world, there is a movement which is like stillness just as there is a motion
which seems to be unmitigated violence. The "incredible slowness" of the
heath, only serves to make more graphic the "catastrophic dash" which
ends the lives of Eustacia and Wildeve. And after the "catastrophic dash"
—"eternal rigidity."

The tragic tension between human and heath, between motion and
repose, between the organic drive away from the inorganic and, what
turns out to be the same thing, the drive to return to the inorganic, provides Hardy with the radical structure of his finest work. The human
struggle against—and temporary departure from—the level stillness of
the heath, is part of that struggle between the vertical and the horizontal
which is a crucial part of Hardy's vision. We read of the "oppressive
horizontality" of the heath, and when Eustacia comes to the time of her
death Hardy describes her position in such a way that it echoes the first
time we saw her, and completes the pattern of her life. She returns to one
of those ancient earthen grave mounds, called barrows. "Eustacia at length
reached Rainbarrow, and stood still there to think . . . she sighed bitterly
and ceased to stand erect, gradually crouching down under the umbrella as
if she were drawn into the Barrow by a hand from underneath." Her
period of motion is over; her erect status above the flatness of the heath
terminates at the same moment: she is, as it were, drawn back into the
undifferentiated levelness of the earth from which she emerged. At the
same time, you will remember, Susan is tormenting and burning a wax
effigy of Eustacia, so that while she seems to be sinking back into the earth
Hardy can also write "the effigy of Eustacia was melting to nothing." She
is losing her distinguishing outline and features. Hardy describes elsewhere
how a woman starts to "lose her own margin" when working the fields.
Human life is featured and contoured life; yet the erosion of feature and
contour seems to be a primal activity of that "featureless convexity" of the
heath, of the earth itself.

This feeling of the constant attrition, and final obliteration, of the
human shape and all human structures, permeates Hardy's work. Inter-
viewed about Stonehenge he commented that "it is a matter of wonder
that the erection has stood so long," adding however that "time nibbles

year after year" at the structure. Just so he will write of a wind "which seemed to gnaw at the corners of the house"; of "wooden posts rubbed to a glossy smoothness by the flanks of infinite cows and calves of bygone years." His work is full of decaying architecture, and in *The Woodlanders* there is a memorable picture of the calves roaming in the ruins of Sherton Castle, "cooling their thirsty tongues by licking the quaint Norman carving, which glistened with the moisture." It is as though time, and all the rest of the natural order, conspired to eat away and erase all the structures and features associated with the human presence on, or intrusion into, the planet. Of one part of the heath Hardy says, in a sentence of extraordinarily succinct power, "There had been no obliteration, because there had been no tending." Tess working at Flintcomb-Ash in a landscape which is "a complexion without features," and Tess running after Angel, "a moving spot intruding on the white facuity," is a visible paradigm of the terms of human life — a spot of featured animation moving painfully across a vast featureless repose. Like Eustacia, and like her wounded horse Prince, having remained upright as long as possible, she, too, simply "ceases to stand erect" and lies down on the flat sacrificial stone, as though offering herself not only up to the sun which tended her, but to the obliterating earth, the horizontal inertia of which she had disturbed.

Life is movement, and movement leads to confusion. Tess's instinct is for placidity, she recoils from rapid movements. Yet at crucial times she finds herself in men's carriages or men' machines. She has to drive her father's cart to market and Prince is killed. Alec forces her into his dogcart which he drives recklessly at great speed. Of Tess we read "the least irregularity of motion startled her" and Alec at this point is disturbing and shaking up blood which will only be stilled in death. Angel, by contrast, takes Tess to the wedding in a carriage which manages to suggest something brutal, punitive, and funereal all at once — "It had stout wheelspokes, and heavy felloes, a great curved bed, immense straps and springs, and a pole like a battering-ram." All these man-made conveyances, together with the ominous train, and that "tyrant" the threshing machine, seem to threaten Tess. And yet she is bound to be involved in travelling, and dangerous motion, because she has no home. At the beginning the parson telling Tess's father about his noble lineage says an ominous thing. to Jack's question, "Where do we d'Urbervilles live?" he answers: "You don't live anywhere. You are extinct—as a county family." Tess does not live anywhere. The one home she finds, Angel turns her out of. That is why she is bound to succumb to Alec. He provides a place but not a home. Alec takes her to Sandbourne, a place of "detached mansions," the very reverse of a community. It is a "pleasure city," "a glittering novelty," a place of meretricious fashion and amusement. "'Tis all lodging-houses here." This is the perfect place for the modern, deracinated Alec. It is no place at all for Tess, "a cottage girl." But we have seen her uprooted, forced to the roads, ejected from houses, knocking on doors which remain closed to her; we have seen the process by which she has become an exhausted helpless prey who is finally bundled off to a boarding house. Her spell in this place is a drugged interlude; she seems finally to have come to that state of catatonic trance which has been anticipated in previous episodes.

Angel realises that "Tess had spiritually ceased to recognize the body before him as hers—allowing it to drift, like a corpse upon the current, in a direction dissociated from its living will." Tess has been so "disturbed" by irregularities of motion, so pulled in different directions, that she really is sick, split, half dead. Hardy was very interested in this sort of split person —for instance, people with primitive instincts and modern nerves, as he says in another book—and we can see that Tess is subjected to too many different pressures, not to say torments, ever to achieve a felicitous wholeness of being.

This brings me to a problem I mentioned earlier. We see Tess suffering, apparently doomed to suffer; destroyed by two men, by society, by the sun outside her and the blood inside her. And we are tempted to ask, what is Hardy's vision of the *cause* of this tale of suffering. Throughout the book Hardy stresses that Tess is damned, and damn herself, according to man-made laws which are as arbitrary as they are cruel. He goes out of his way to show how Nature seems to disdain, ignore or make mockery of the laws which social beings impose on themselves. The fetish of chastity is a ludicrous aberration in a world which teems and spills with such promiscuous and far-flung fertility every year (not to say a brutal caricature of human justice in that what was damned in the woman was condoned in the man). So, if the book was an attempt to show an innocent girl who is destroyed by society though justified by Nature, Hardy could certainly have left the opposition as direct and as simple as that. Social laws hang Tess; and Nature admits no such laws. But it is an important part of the book that we feel Nature itself turning against Tess, so that we register something approaching a sadism of *both* the man-made *and* the natural directed against her. If she is tortured by the man-made threshing machine, she is also crushed by the forge of the sun; the cold negating metal in Angel is also to be found in the "steely stars"; the pangs of guilt which lacerate her are matched by the "glass splinters" of rain which penetrate her at Flintcomb-Ash. Perhaps to understand this feeling of almost universal opposition which grows throughout the book, we should turn to some of Hardy's own words, when he talks of "the universal harshness . . . the harshness of the position towards the temperament, of the means towards the aims, of today towards yesterday, of hereafter towards today." When he meditates on the imminent disappearance of the d'Urberville family he says, "so does Time ruthlessly destroy his own romances." This suggests a universe of radical opposition, working to destroy what it works to create, crushing to death what it coaxes into life. From this point of view society only appears as a functioning part of a larger process whereby the vertical returns to the horizontal, motion lapses into stillness and structure cedes to the unstructured. The policemen appear as the sun rises: Tess is a sacrifice to both, to all of them. Hardy's vision is tragic and penetrates far deeper than specific social anomalies. One is more inclined to think of Sophocles than, say, Zola, when reading Hardy. The vision is tragic because he shows an ordering of existence in which nature turns against itself, in which the sun blasts what it blesses, in which all the hopeful explorations of life turn out to have been a circuitous peregrination towards death. "All things are born to be diminished" said Pericles at the time of Sophocles; and Hardy's comparable feeling that all things are tended to be obliterated, reveals a Sophoclean grasp of the bed-rock ironies of existence.

Tess is the living demonstration of these tragic ironies. That is why she who is raped lives to be hanged; why she who is so physically beautiful feels guilt at "inhabiting the fleshly tabernacle with which Nature had endowed her"; why she who is a fertile source of life comes to feel that "birth itself was an ordeal of degrading personal compulsion, whose gratuitousness nothing in the result seemed to justify." It is why she attracts the incompatible forces represented by Alec and Angel. It is why she who is a lover is also a killer. Tess is gradually crucified on the oppugnant ironies of circumstance and existence itself, ironies which centre, I have suggested, on the fact of blood, that basic stuff which starts the human spot moving across the white vacuity. Blood, and the spilling of blood; which in one set of circumstances can mean sexual passion and the creation of life, and in another can mean murderous passion and death—two forms of "red" energy intimately related—this is the substance of Tess's story. And why should it all happen to her? You can say, as some people in the book say fatalistically, "It was to be." Or you could go through the book and try to work out how Hardy apportions the blame—a bit on Tess, a bit on society, a bit on religion, a bit on heredity, a bit on the Industrial Revolution, a bit on the men who abuse her, a bit on the sun and the stars, and so on. But Hardy does not work in this way. More than make us judge, Hardy makes us see; and in looking for some explanation of why all this should happen to Tess, our eyes finally settle on that red ribbon marking out the little girl in the white dress, which already foreshadows the red blood stain on the white ceiling. In her beginning is her end. It is the oldest of truths, but it takes a great writer to make us experience it again in all its awesome mystery.

Hardy specifically rejected the idea of offering any theory of the universe. In his General Preface to his works, he said "Nor is it likely, indeed, that imaginative writings extending over more than forty years would exhibit a coherent scientific theory of the universe even if it had been attempted—of that universe concerning which Spencer owns to the 'paralyzing thought' that possibly there exists no comprehension of it anywhere. But such objectless consistency never has been attempted." Hardy "theorizes" far less than Lawrence, but certain images recur which serve to convey his sense of life —its poignancy and its incomprehensibility —more memorably than any overt statement. Death, the sudden end of brilliance and movement, occupied a constant place in his thoughts. "The most prosaic man becomes a poem when you stand by his grave and think of him" he once wrote; and the strange brightness of ephemeral creatures is something one often meets in his fiction—pictorially, not philosophically. "Gnats, knowing nothing of their brief glorification, wandered across the shimmer of this pathway, irradiated as if they bore fire within them, then passed out of its line, and were quite extinct." Compare with that the description of the girls returning from the dance: "and as they went there moved onward with them . . . a circle of opalized light, formed by the moon's rays upon the glistening sheet of dew. Each pedestrian could see no halo but his or her own." Hardy is often to be found stressing the ephemeral nature of life —"independent worlds of ephemerons were passing their time in mad carousal," "ephemeral creatures, took up their positions where only a year ago other had stood in their place when these were nothing more than germs and inorganic particles"—and it often seems that the ephemeral fragments of moving life are also like bubbles of light, temporary illuminations of an encroaching darkness. One of the great scenes in all of Hardy is in *The Return of the Native* when Wildeve and Venn, the reddleman, gamble at night on the heath. Their lantern makes a little circle of light which draws things out of the darkness towards it. "The light of the candle had by this time attracted heath-flies, moths and other winged creatures of night, which floated round the lantern, flew into the flame, or beat about the faces of the two players." Much more suggestively as they continue to throw dice; "they were surrounded by dusky forms about four feet high, standing a few paces beyond the rays of the lantern. A moment's inspection revealed that the encircling figures were heath-croppers, their heads being all towards the players, at whom they gazed intently." When a moth extinguishes the candle, Wildeve gathers glow worms and puts them on the stone on which they are playing. "The incongruity between the men's deeds and their environment was great. Amid the soft juicy vegetation of the hollow in which they sat, the motionless and the uninhabited solitude, intruded the chink of guineas, the rattle of dice, the exclamations of the reckless players." Again, it is one of those scenes which seems to condense a whole vision of human existence — a strange activity in a small circle of light, and all round them the horses of the night noiselessly gathering at the very perimeter. And in *Tess of the D'Urbervilles* Hardy develops this scene into a metaphor of great power. He is describing how Tess's love for Angel sustains her: "it enveloped her as a photosphere, irradiated her into forgetfulness of her past sorrows, keeping back the gloomy spectres that would persist in their attempts to touch her — doubt, fear, moodiness, care, shame. She knew that they were waiting like wolves just outside the circumscribing light, but she had long spells of power to keep them in hungry subjection there . . . She walked in brightness, but she knew that in the background those shapes of darkness were always spread."

I have singled out this image not only because I think there is something quintessentially Hardyan in it, but also because I think it is an image which profoundly influenced D. H. Lawrence. Here is a final quotation, taken from the culmination of perhaps his greatest novel, *The Rainbow*. Ursula is trying to clarify her sense of her own presence in the world.

> This world in which she lived was like a circle lighted by a lamp. This lighted area, lit up by man's completest consciousness, she thought was all the world: that here all was disclosed for ever. Yet all the time, within the darkness she had been aware of points of light, like the eyes of wild beasts, gleaming, penetrating, vanishing. And her soul had acknowledged in a great heave of terror only the outer darkness. This inner circle of light in which she lived and moved, wherein the trains rushed and the factories ground out their machine-produce and the

plants and the animals worked by the light of science and knowledge, suddenly it seemed like the area under an arc lamp, wherein the moths and children played in the security of blinding light, not even knowing there was any darkness, because they stayed in the light.

But she could see the glimmer of dark movement just out of range, she saw the eyes of the wild beast gleaming from the darkness, watching the vanity of the camp fire and the sleepers; she felt the strange, foolish vanity of the camp, which said "Beyond our light and our order there is nothing," turning their faces always inwards toward the sinking fire of illuminating consciousness, which comprised sun and stars, and the Creator, and the System of Righteousness, ignoring always the vast shapes that wheeled round about, with half-revealed shapes lurking on the edge. . . .

Nevertheless the darkness wheeled round about, with grey shadow-shapes of wild beasts, and also with dark shadow-shapes of the angels, whom the light fenced out, as it fenced out the more familiar beasts of darkness.

Lawrence, more insistent as to the torments and sterilities of consciousness, confidently ascribes positive values to the shapes prowling around the perimeter of the circle of light. But Lawrence's *interpretation*—itself an act of consciousness—of the population of the dark, is only something overlayed on the *situation*, that irreducible configuration which is to be found, I suggest, at the heart of Hardy's work. "She walked in brightness, but she knew that in the background those shapes of darkness were always spread."

"The Perfection of Species" and Hardy's Tess

Bruce Johnson

A curious, almost geological metaphor is submerged in the early chapters of *Tess*, suggesting time or history as though it were geological strata, earlier strata occasionally visible in the present but all strata necessary for a sense of the present. Thus in the opening scene the two interwoven keynotes are John's discovery of his noble descent, with its resonance of ancestral seats and lead coffins, and the club-walking—the parade of women all dressed in white and carrying a peeled willow wand and flowers. Hardy clearly implies that the women's club has lost contact with the original sexual and mythic implications of the May festival, or "cerelia" (his term). It is a rite of sexuality and fertility, as the peeled willow wand suggests, and perhaps of innocence in the participation not only of maidens but also of older, experienced women. The white clothing worn by all confirms what must have been the ceremony's ancient ability to raise its participants to a state of pagan grace. The "ideal" whiteness of the costumes survives despite the actual variety among them, some actually "of a cadaverous tint" on close examination. The ceremony has been inherited, Hardy reminds us, in a "disguised form."

This is very like the analysis Frazer makes in *The Golden Bough*. A contemporary ceremony is examined as though it were a living fossil. The Catholic Mass? Surely man has eaten the god for eons. The murder of the priest in the grove? We have lost the meaning, but it can be recovered through penetration of the strata that comprise its particular formation and

From *Nature and the Victorian Imagination.* © 1977 by The Regents of the University of California. The University of California Press, 1977.

by a comparative mythology that aids that penetration. Hardy's suggestion that Tess's club no longer has access to the mythic aspect of its dance and parade is a common enough maneuver in his work; one can hardly stroll down a lane in Wessex but it becomes a Roman road, and the hills are so often tumuli that one feels himself in an atmosphere where the whole countryside becomes symbolic of an infinitely stratified sense of place.

If this is Hardy's attitude toward the recovery of a mythic past, why has he woven the club-walking in with John's discovery of his ancestry? The two events seem to invite comparison. Indeed, the question of Tess's subsequent relation to her d'Urberville past is immediately raised. Should she have been—after the name of her first important ancestor—a pagan in some sense? Has she really come "home" to Stonehenge? The most naïve explanation for Hardy's association of these two potential "recoveries" of the past is that his attitude toward the club-walking is ultimately the same as that toward Tess's (if not John's) recovery of her past: she is better off with it, and, in fact, it may offer some clue as to "what Tess might have been." It is inviting to suppose Hardy felt that any mind aware of its historical evolution is wiser, if not happier, and better equipped to deal with the immense indifference of things.

Just as the ancient significances of the club-walking flicker beneath its contemporary surface, so do Tess's earlier stages occasionally flash forth: "Phases of her childhood lurked in her aspect still. As she walked along today, for all her bouncing, handsome womanliness, you could sometimes see her twelfth year in her cheeks, or her ninth sparkling from her eyes; and even her fifth would flit over the curves of her mouth now and then." An ordinary enough observation, but entirely in keeping with the concern for the detectable past not only *in* the present but also comprising it in some organically geological sense. Somehow the present—1880—militates against the stratified past as it is felt even by Tess's otherwise uncomprehending mother, who carries a "fast-perishing lumber of superstitions, folk-lore, dialect, and orally transmitted ballads"; Joan is contrasted with Tess, whose "trained National teachings and Standard knowledge under an infinitely Revised Code" seem to eliminate any such feeling.

Tess resists the recovery of her past, largely because she sees it, as we do, as social climbing and pretension. She examines the phoney d'Urberville's face for precisely the "vestiges" or "survivals" (to use the appropriate late-nineteenth-century anthropological terms) that might have been detected in the club-walking: "She had dreamed of an aged and dignified face, the sublimation of all the d'Urberville lineaments, furrowed with incarnate memories representing in hieroglyphics the centuries of her family's and England's history." Hardy's attitude, indeed Tess's own attitude, is that such hieroglyphics should be read, whatever untoward suggestions they may harbor. "Our names," she says, "are worn away to Durbeyfield," suggesting not only the weathering of an engraving but also the slow geological evolution that erodes landscapes.

It is no accident that the modern country estate of the bastardized Stoke-d'Urbervilles lies adjacent to the contrastingly "primeval" Chase, "wherein Druidical mistletoe was still found on aged oaks, and where enormous yew trees, not planted by the hand of man, grew as they had grown when they were pollarded for bows." It is characteristically Hardian that the mistletoe is "Druidical," for he sees his country folk as the result of a more-or-less steady evolution from Druidical culture, Christianity representing an interference with such evolution. Christianity, in fact, has made the meaning of the Maypole dance inaccessible even to the dancers. Hardy seems to associate the ability to be in touch with primeval, pagan meanings with the ability to be in touch with the emotional, primitive sources of one's own being; the buried geological or archeological, or even paleontological, metaphors of his work really imply an ideal model of consciousness, an awareness of the primeval energies that have shaped even the mind's outward topography.

The intellectual influence behind Hardy's thinking was of course not Freud, but rather such people as the geologist Lyell, the so-called evolutionary anthropologists (Tylor, Frazer, Lewis Henry Morgan), and Darwin. Among those who are generally agreed to have influenced Hardy, Schopenhauer's analysis of will, with its often incredible resemblance to Freud's sense of the unconscious, must come first to mind. It is Hardy's rather special understanding of Darwin, however, that becomes important for my argument, since it was apparently from Darwin, and specifically from the *Origin of Species*, that Hardy took his most delicate sense of the relationship between past and present.

The well-known "Nature" passage that describes Tess's walks after her first return home has been used to argue Hardy's affinity with Schopenhauer. Hardy's attitude toward Nature would seem to be that it is involved with human nature through the common Will (e.g., the animation of Egdon Heath in *The Return of the Native*). But if we set aside the philosophical background, the passages become rather more complicated and less Schopenhauerian than has been imagined. The particular passage in *Tess*—"On these lonely hills and dales her quiescent glide was of a piece with the elements she moved in"—and the following two paragraphs, affirm more than that "the world is only a psychological phenomenon."

Tess animates Nature with an attitude or mood that is antipathetic to it: she feels she is "guilty" and that Nature is "innocent." But, says Hardy, both she *and* Nature are innocent: "She had been made to break an accepted social law, but no law known to the environment in which she found herself such an anomaly." Although she creates the world of Nature as a psychological phenomenon, the passage suggests that there is a more "real" Nature that her psychological perceptions cannot touch, a Nature not susceptible to judgments of guilt that must be called innocent. The implication, as generations of critics have noted, is that ideally Tess should not feel guilty. Immediately before this passage we have met the country zealot who goes around daubing his religious "texts" on every likely barn or stile; Tess had felt his categorical condemnations to be "horrible," and Hardy now contrasts them with the sun worship of her ancestors:

> The sun, on account of the mist, had a curious sentient, personal look, demanding the masculine pronoun for its adequate expression. His present aspect, coupled with the lack of all human forms in the scene, explained the old-time heliolatries in a moment. One could feel that a saner religion had never prevailed under the sky. The luminary was a golden-haired, beaming, mild-eyed, God-like creature, gazing down in the vigor and intentness of youth upon an earth that was brimming with interest for him.

Here Hardy implies that Christianity's capacity for creating guilt is unfortunate and that the old heliolatry had no such intent—that it must have been in this regard an unusually sane religion. Unlike Hardy's usual conception of deities, the sun-god finds earth "brimming with interest for him."

In short, any ability in Tess to make contact with earlier, more primitive, though not necessarily unconscious, levels of her mind might have diminished her sense of guilt. Her "Druidical" past is associated, not primarily with oak forests and mistletoe, but with Stonehenge and the worship of the sun. The final crushing irony of the novel is that as Tess lies on the altar (a pagan come home), the first constable rises just where the sun should have risen. Tess is sacrificed to the restrictions and punishments of modern society rather than to the sun. The sun suggests a higher awareness: an ancient organically evolved consciousness that dynamically retains in the present remnants of the past, much in the sense that Tylor, Darwin, and Frazer had established.

The emphasis early in the novel is on Tess as an essentially natural woman. Hardy describes her reaping: "A field-man is a personality afield; a field-woman is a portion of the field; she has somehow lost her own margin, imbibed the essence of her surrounding, and assimilated herself with it." Although he implies that Tess has not yet developed an ideal sort of consciousness, she apparently shares with her sex a *disposition* to discount social convention and to recognize in Nature a force indifferent to it. Earlier she had animated Nature with her own guilt feelings; now she recognizes that despite these feelings "the trees were just as green as before; the birds sang and the sun shown just as clearly now as ever. The familiar surroundings had not darkened because of her grief, nor sickened because of her pain." Hardy speculates how she would feel about her seduction and child if she were free from the pressures of social convention: "Moreover, alone on a desert island would she have been wretched at what had happened to her? Not greatly." Nature, it seems, is not merely a psychological phenomenon but is also a self-sufficient entity whose fundamental qualities Tess often demonstrates. Nature sustains her, and these manifold references to her naturalness are apparently by way of preparation for the christening scene. What happens there is very revealing of Tess's psychology. Ready to take on herself a responsibility that ordinarily belongs to convention and church organization, she simultaneously respects the letter of convention while she violates the spirit of it. Her naturalness and spontaneity are evident; she functions, as Nature does, with characteristic self-sufficiency. At this point in the novel we can only make informed guesses as to what such a "natural" tendency may mean; but it has to do with the recognition of Tess as a pagan, a motif that runs throughout the novel, and in a sense closes it.

What is certain is that Tess's recovery is associated with Nature: "The recuperative power which pervaded organic nature was surely not denied to maidenhead alone"; when a "particularly fine spring came round . . . it moved her, as it moved the wild animals, and made her passionate to go." The last paragraph before "Phase the Third—the Rally" indicates that this natural recovery is equally drawn from her ancestors and their country. The parallel established is between the natural resurgence of her "invincible instinct toward self-delight" and the potential recovery of her d'Urberville past. These two "recoveries" run side by side as though they were analogous to one another.

Are both of these necessary for the truly "pagan" Tess? "All the while she wondered if *any strange good thing* might come of her being in her ancestral land; and some spirit rose within her *as the sap in the twigs*" (my italics). The syntax couples the recovery of the ancestral past with the natural identity; the one seems to touch off what Hardy can only express in the utterly natural flow of sap. We are tempted to read that phrase "strange good thing" as entirely ironical, in view of what happens to Tess in the land of her ancestors. But as presented in this paragraph, such is not the tone at all. There is a real chance that the land of her ancestors might hold some "strange good thing"—as good as Tess's increasing awareness of her natural identity.

Never having been in this country, Tess nonetheless "felt akin to the landscape" and finds in the distance the location of her ancestral tombs, her "useless ancestors." "She had no admiration for them now; she almost hated them for the dance they had led her; not a thing of all that had been theirs did she retain but the seal and the spoon." The irony is obvious; she inherits far more than the seal and the spoon. Hardy strongly suggests that her ancestors had been crudely misused in John's mercenary quest for kin, and that Tess is indeed a d'Urberville. In seeking to use the d'Urbervilles, as her family had suggested, it is poetic justice that Tess gets only a fake ancestor rather than something of the old frightening vitality and authority.

As she plunges into the vale of Talbothays, Tess chants a Christian canticle, which to Hardy sounds more like a pagan song of joy: "and probably the half-unconscious rapsody was a Fetichistic utterance in a Monotheistic setting; women whose chief companions are the forms and forces of outdoor Nature retain in their souls far more of the pagan fantasy of their remote forefathers than of the systematized religion taught their race at later date." Again we are invited to see Tess in her natural capacity, and once more this familiar motif is associated with the return to the land of her ancestors. Christianity is seen as a thin overlay on an essentially pagan appreciation of natural "forms and forces." The very posts of the dairy barn are presented almost as a fetish, suggesting an apprehension of death and oblivion that competes with Christian ideas: "wooden posts rubbed to a glossy smoothness by the flanks of infinite cows and calves of bygone years, now passed to an oblivion almost inconceivable in its profundity"—a remarkable phrase and one intimating that this "profundity" is available to an un-Christian sensibility. Even the landscape of Talbothays suggests geological metaphors that readily blend into paleontological ones: "Thus they all worked on, encompassed by the vast flat mead which extended to either slope of the valley—a level landscape compounded of old landscapes long forgotten, and, no doubt, differing in character very greatly from the landscape they composed now." This image can stand for Tess's state of mind, for what Hardy wants to cultivate in Tess is a sense of the role those old landscapes play in the present one. The precise mode of their participation in the reality of the present was one of the great late-Victorian issues that crossed the boundaries of a dozen disciplines.

There is every reason to believe that the consciousness of Angel Clare is meant to contrast the potential in Tess that is suggested by the landscape metaphor mentioned above; when he thinks, "what a fresh and virginal daughter of Nature that milk-maid is!", he is far from appreciating the more complex relation of Tess to Nature. Tess is of course close to Nature, as Hardy has so often intimated; but her virginity comprehends the seduction and child and is continually renewed by her undiminished capacity for innocence. All this is like cyclical Nature renewing itself, as was suggested by the May ceremony that opened the novel. Unfortunately, Angel means something conventional by his "virginal" and cannot begin to comprehend the larger and more powerful sense of the word.

His psychology as it is presented in chapter 18 runs counter to the evolutionism of Hardy's landscapes. To Clare, his religion is not an evolving process to be contained in the mind, as Hardy views the landscape — "compounded of old landscapes long forgotten" — it is rather to be ruthlessly pruned of what now seems useless: "an untenable redemptive theolatry." "My whole instinct in matters of religion is toward reconstruction; to quote your favorite Epistle to the Hebrews, 'the removing of those things that are shaken, as of things that are made, that those things which cannot be shaken may remain.'" I suspect that the idea of constructing, or building, or in general *restoring*, religion is uncongenial to Hardy. Angel's cold application of intellect to the evolved body of religion makes it seem too easy to "reconstruct," to subtract and demolish, as though one were working with a badly constructed building. (Hardy's knowledge of architecture and especially of the preservation of churches moved far beyond any such rough-and-ready notions.) Hardy was among those who did not feel it likely or possible that a wholesome ethics could simply be abstracted from "an untenable redemptive theolatry." Whatever else his attitude may have been toward the supernaturalism of Christianity, it was deeply respectful, at times even secularly reverent.

Although Angel is making "close acquaintance with phenomena which he had before known but darkly — the seasons in their moods, morning and evening, night and noon, winds in their different tempers, trees, waters, and mists, shades and silences, and the voices of inanimate things" — he remains an idealist of Nature and speaks to Tess, even if casually, of "pastoral life in ancient Greece." It is a deceptively dreamy remark by Tess about how "souls can be made to go outside our bodies" that first attracts him to her. Angel creates a number of illusions about Tess, the foremost being his notion that she is a child of *his* nature rather than of hers. Nature comes under close examination in these pages, and it is once more coupled with the problem of Tess's inheritance. Several of the most difficult "Nature" passages in the novel are immediately followed by a rather complex revelation of Tess's questioning whether she ought to reveal to Angel her d'Urberville past, the past that she at times so abruptly dismisses as useless.

In one such passage the emphasis is on a psychologized Nature:

> It was a typical summer evening in June, the atmosphere being in such delicate equilibrium and so transmissive that inanimate objects seemed endowed with two or three senses, if not five. There was no distinction between the near and the far, and an auditor felt close to everything within the horizon. The soundlessness impressed her as a positive entity rather than as the mere negation of noise. It was broken by the strumming of strings.

So thoroughly is Nature possessed by the mind of the sensor that what is clearly a sensual preoccupation on Tess's part turns the notes of Angel's distant harp into his body itself: "They [the sounds] had never appealed to her as now, when they wandered in the still air with a stark quality like that of nudity." This passage is immediately followed by the more famous and apparently contradictory Nature passage:

> The outskirt of the garden in which Tess found herself had been left uncultivated for some years, and was now damp and rank with juicy grass which sent up mists of pollen at a touch; and with tall blooming weeds emitting offensive smells—weeds whose red and yellow and purple hues formed a polychrome as dazzling as that of cultivated flowers. She went stealthily as a cat through this profusion of growth, gathering cuckoo-spittle on her skirts, cracking snails that were underfoot, straining her hands with thistle-milk and slug-slime, and rubbing off upon her naked arms sticky blights which, though snow-white on the apple-tree trunks, made madder stains on her skin; thus she drew quite near to Clare, still unobserved of him.

Our senses come alive to the sticky objectionableness of Nature in this fecund yet decaying garden. Whatever symbolism the garden may suggest (and readers have had a feast of meanings almost since the moment the novel was published), we clearly smell, touch, see, and feel some general vague corruption here. Who can say with what sense we apprehend the snails cracked underfoot, the mists of rank pollen, the deceptiveness of the brightly colored weeks, and the "sticky blights" that stain Tess's skin but are snow-white on the tree?

This is a distinctly Hardian Garden of Eden: Nature is untended by any god, and this Angel is certainly no god's messenger. Here, rather, is Darwin's "tangled bank," although the emphasis is undeveloped. Though she cannot see it, *this* is what really lies before Tess. Her mind transforms the scene; she "was conscious of neither space nor time." Her soul passes out of her body, as she has suggested it could, gazing at stars. "She undulated upon the thin notes of the second-hand harp." Even the pollen "seemed to be [Angel's] notes visible," the clammy dampness "the weeping of the garden's sensibility." One notes the gratuitous "second-hand," and concludes that along with all the other evidence this constitutes a critical emphasis on the difference between "reality" and Tess's at-this-moment transcendent sensibility. The garden is fecund and sensuous, in keeping with her perception of Angel's harp notes as nudity itself, but it is also deceptive, as is her transcendent state of mind.

Hardy stresses what is objectively *there* as a kind of dramatic irony, even a warning about the nature of the relationship developing between Angel and Tess. Angel's talent for bringing out this transcendent quality in Tess runs counter to the different relationship with Nature that is equally possible for her, a relationship suggested by her sense of having come "home" to Stonehenge, by her being a very old creature rather than, as she says, a new one: "The insight afforded into Clare's character suggested to her that it was largely owing to her supposed untraditional newness that she had won interest in his eyes." This is the beginning of one of the most phenomenologically primitive issues of the whole novel: the virtually metaphysical differences between old and new. Thus the long discussions in these pages about Clare's distaste for old families and Tess's refusal of his offer to teach her history: "Because what's the use of learning that I am one of a long row only—finding out that there is set down in some old book someone just like me, and to know that I shall only act her part; making me sad, that's all. The best is not to remember that your nature and your past doings have been just like thousands' and thousands' and that your coming life and doings'll be like thousands' and thousands'."

The awareness of the past that Hardy has implied through the landscape metaphor leads not at all to the conclusions Tess has reached. Ironically, a moment after she has thus rejected the past she unwittingly echoes Job by saying that while she does not want historical knowledge, she "shouldn't mind learning why—why the sun do shine on the just and the unjust alike." Hardy presumably rejects the "long row" metaphor in favor of something like the geological or paleontological one. Even Tess is momentarily persuaded that she ought to mention her forebears to a gentleman like Angel, to show she is not spurious d'Urberville, "but true d'Urberville to the bone." In view of Hardy's apparent flirtation with the idea that inherited character was in fact destiny, this sounds entirely deterministic. Such an interpretation, however, fails to explain the conjoining of the Nature motifs with all the d'Urberville material and makes of Tess's story a long row indeed.

Angel's taste, however, is for the "new" man or woman. We are told he has "great hopes" for the lad named Matt who never heard he had a surname and supposed this was so because his folks hadn't been established long enough. Matt's namelessness is another kind of nudity, if not some kind of deracination. Tess responds wittily on hearing this report of Clare, thinking that her family was so "unusually old as almost to have gone round the circle and become a new one." But it is not "untraditional newness" that Hardy wants, even if Clare does.

While Clare calls Tess Artemis and Demeter, far from connecting her genuinely with any traditions, this serves only to empty her of any personal identity in favor of a "visionary essence of woman." Tess's answer is the corrective, "Call me Tess," although as a rule she submits to this attempt at transforming a human being into an abstract and transcendent principle. It is almost as though Clare, having lost belief in the transcendence of his religion, has tried to relocate such transcendence in Tess. If his Christianity has lost its innocence, Tess will be made to resurrect the old feelings. To say that Tess cannot endure this burden because she has a secret sin is to miss the point. No woman, much less Tess, could ultimately have borne it. It is fitting that such ethereal touches as Tess looking "ghostly, as if she were merely a soul at large," and the dew touching her eyelashes as though it were seed pearls, should be undercut by the sun that shows her to be a "dazzlingly fair dairymaid only."

If he still tends to abstract Tess into something she is not, Angel nonetheless is capable of seeing, in a sensuous moment after his return, "the red interior of her mouth as if it had been a snake's." The sexual details of her waking body are simply not accepted by Angel for what they are. Hardy, representing Angel's point of view, says: "It was a moment when a woman's soul is more incarnate than at any other time; when the most spiritual beauty bespeaks itself flesh; and sex takes the outside place in the presentation." (One cannot resist imagining how D. H. Lawrence would have written this paragraph.) Even in so sensuous a moment sex takes last place. Angel still sees Tess as something of a sexual threat, but primarily as a threat to his immaculate entherealizing process. To him, her sensuous and emotional reality is made the abstract essence of a mythologized Nature.

When Tess and Angel deliver the milk to the railway station they pass "an old manor house of Caroline Date," which Angel tells her was one of the seats of the ancient d'Urberville family. Thus begins an intensification of references, already frequent, to her "inheritance." Angel's interest in old families, even before Tess tells him about her ancestry, seems strange in one so dedicated to the new. After her revelation of d'Urberville blood, his behavior, in view of his taste for newness in her, is even more remarkable. He even contrives to spend their wedding night in a d'Urberville house, allowing Hardy to cast the events of those few days against the melodramatic presence of the two d'Urberville women whose portraits cannot be removed from the old manor. No doubt these two portraits and the reiterated story of the d'Urberville coach constitute (along with many other details) a kind of Gothic curse on the family, a "ballad" element that is not skillfully handled or very meaningful. Critics have often said so. Yet no one has adequately explained why the d'Urberville material *is* so pervasive and so often brought into pregnant if not readily comprehensible association with other important motifs. For example, the same page that contains Angel's reference to the old manor offers a brilliant description of the modern world, in the image of the train as some reluctant creature extending its "feelers" into the primeval countryside and withdrawing, "as if what it touched had been uncongenial." When the light of the engine illuminates Tess, "no object could have looked more foreign to the gleaming cranks and wheels than this unsophisticated girl, with the round, bare arms, the rainy face and hair, the suspended attitude of a friendly leopard at pause, the print gown of no date or fashion, and the cotton bonnet dropping on her brow." Just before, Angel has said, "There is something very sad in the extinction of a family of renown, even if it was a fierce, domineering, feudal renown." That Tess should possess the attitude of a "friendly leopard" suggests a connection between these identifications.

Tess is indeed fierce. She has the leopard's instinctive capacity to kill naturally, even with composure. Her love for Angel is fierce, even if forbearance is its outward mode; her loyalty to him is fierce, despite his abandonment of her. It is almost as though in calling Tess "natural," Hardy is insisting on a distinctly Darwinian flavor to the word. He was, after all, steeped in Darwin and Huxley and Herbert Spencer. As David Lodge has suggested, the characteristics of the garden in which Tess listens rapt to

Angel's harp may be attributable to Tess. Playing on the word "madder," he rightly concludes that Tess herself is consonant with the "unconstrained nature" of the garden and that "the force of this connection between Tess and the natural world is to suggest that 'mad' passionate, nonethical quality of her sensibility." If she moves "stealthily as a cat" through this garden, it is as the leopard rather than the household tabby—not that she is about to prey on Angel, but certainly in her capacity for passionate reaction. This is the reputation of the d'Urberville family, even if, as Angel suggests, it once manifested itself as crass "self-seeking." The readily apparent differences between the old d'Urbervilles and Tess begin to pale when we recognize the unconstrained naturalness they share. In the d'Urbervilles the results are none too pleasant, but Hardy must present a potent antidote to Angel's view of naturalness—one might say his *myth* of naturalness.

There can be little doubt that David J. DeLaura's view of Angel is correct: that he is associated with Matthew Arnold and that his "sin, like that of the later Arnold, is precisely his imperfect modernism, his slavery in the ethical sphere to 'custom and conventionality.'" For Hardy, Arnold had fatally compromised himself in the seventies by his mediating theo-logical position, metaphysically agnostic but emotionally and morally traditional and "Christian." What Hardy wants is "a greater honesty in confronting (to use Arnold's own youthful phrase) 'the modern situation in its true *blankness* and *barrenness*, and *unpoetrylessness*.'" To do this Hardy requires a life that does not rely on "comforting theistic palliatives" of the sort that Angel locates in his myth of Tess's naturalness. He is, indeed, almost Wordsworthian in what values he expects to derive from Tess's natural origins. Those ethics he expects to loose from the background of "redemptive theolatry" represent less Hebraism than a kind of loosely conceived Hellenism and a "culture" that he proudly cultivates apart from the formal theological basis it has in his two brothers. Why else has Hardy given us the detailed background of old Mr. Clare's refusal to educate Angel at Oxford and Angel's reaction to this?

Yet Angel's carefully dissociated "culture" does not exempt him from applying to Tess the most hopelessly bourgeois double standard. His Hellenism and his culture are ashes compared to the natural depths from which she draws her fidelity and her determination to survive. Angel is deliberately set up as a possible answer to the ache of modernism, and he fails utterly, whatever combination of intellectual positions of the 1870s and 1880s he may be seen to represent. DeLaura concludes that the source of value Hardy finally offers is "the simple endorsement (predictive of Lawrence) of freer relations between men and women unhampered by the stifling and unnatural standards of a dying civilization." To him, the major ethical contrast, "pervasive in *Tess* and central in *Jude* is a simple one between an unspecified 'Nature,' evidently as the norm of some more genuine and personal ethical mode, and 'Civilization,' identified with social law, convention, and in the last analysis the moral and intellectual constraints of Christianity." De Laura thinks this feeling for Nature in Hardy is disguised sentimentalism and calls it "Wordsworthian."

I have been arguing that, on the contrary, it is far from being an un-developed idea, entirely unsentimental, and at the roots of Tess's paganism. Culture and its rationalism are a veneer, as Hardy often shows and says. But there are two kinds of culture: the sort Angel proudly cultivates and the kind that is closer to a modern anthropologist's definition. Tess is in-volved in her own culture and not simply in some direct, palpable contact with Nature. One remembers in this connection Dorothy Van Ghent's speculations about the importance of sheer "earth" in this novel. Still, her conclusion that Tess springs from "instinctivism," "fatalism," and "magic" seems to be in conflict with the evidence that Hardy wanted to make Tess an aristocrat, a true d'Urberville.

We may well emphasize one entry in Hardy's autobiography: "New Year's thought. A perception of the FAILURE OF THINGS to be what they are meant to be, lends them, in place of the intended interest, a new and greater interest of an unintended kind." The evolutionary conscious-ness that was so vital a part of the late nineteenth-century sensibility did not of course look at the "old landscapes" inherent in the present, or at fossils come to light in some dig, as dead and mere curiosities. Such fossil material was more often seen in current, living society or mind as "sur-vivals" that, under the analysis of Frazer or even Freud, were seen posi-tively as helping to *explain* the enigmatic configuration of the present. There is a spacious ambience in the thinking of many Victorians (not the least of them George Eliot) that allows them to make analogies between "old landscapes," fossils, cultural survivals (the "cerelia" that begins *Tess*) and, certainly in the case of Tess, family histories. In *Tess* the family history is like that of the old landscapes. Far from there being a real conflict in the reader's tripartite identification of Tess as a child of Nature, of the folk culture, and of the long d'Urberville inheritance, to Hardy's way of think-ing the d'Urberville psychic inheritance was itself subject to great and natural evolutionary forces that make it part of Tess's consciousness as much, and in the same way, as the old landscapes are part of Var Vale. Tess's aristocratic family sinks back into a soil of folk culture somewhat in the same sense that there is always a fundamental "ground" from which any number of possible landscapes may evolve. But this ground (we may even elicit here some of the connotations that word has in Gestalt psychology) is always altered by the noble families that have apparently sunk back into it. (Tess is told of many "vestiges" in the debased names of milkmaids and village lads.) And of course the process is being permanently altered if not destroyed by the gradual loss of true folk culture. The cities expand; folk leave the land never to return.

Hardy's continual association of Tess's naturalness with her d'Urberville inheritance betrays a hidden but potent bias: to be natural is somehow to be *like* the violent, self-sufficient, proud d'Urbervilles and very little like Nature as Angel perceives it. Furthermore, the "natural" d'Urberville quality in Tess is hers not simply as part of a "long row," but as the old landscapes are part of the presently tranquil Var Vale. Hardy, like many late Victorians, was beginning to be especially sensitive to the record of violence and upheaval that lay buried, but still armed, in the rocks. The strata were not only telling an old story but also revealing a present process.

It would appear, then, that one of the keys to *Tess* lies precisely in Hardy's understanding of this crucial late-Victorian concept of the relation between past and present. We begin to appreciate its full flavor by realizing how much actual historiography there is in these early anthropologists—especially in Frazer and Tylor. Henceforth it will be very difficult for historians to write without borrowing some late-Victorian ideas about evolutionary culture, ideas that come in large part from the evolutionary anthropologists. Similarly, contemporary historians nearly always assume the fully relativistic (rather than evolutionary) model of culture developed by modern anthropologists. Even Toynbee is essentially a cultural relativist.

For Hardy, it is obviously Darwin's ideas that are crucial, yet the details of Hardy's vivid reaction to Darwin have been largely a mystery. That Hardy emphasized the evolutionary connections among all life (the relatedness of man and "lower" forms) over the "survival of the fittest," is a point insufficiently emphasized by those who discuss him. It was made some fifteen years ago in an article by Elliott B. Gose, Jr., who quotes the crucial passage from Hardy's notebook: "The discovery of the law of evolution which revealed that all organic creatures are of one family, shifted the center of altruism from humanity to the whole conscious world collectively." Equally important is Hardy's note written before he began *Tess*: "Altruism, or the Golden Rule, or whatever 'Love your Neighbor as Yourself' may be called, will ultimately be brought about I think by the pain we see in others reacting on ourselves, as if we and they were a part of

one body. Mankind, in fact, may be and possibly will be viewed as members of one corporeal frame." Whether Comte or Schopenhauer is more
nearly reflected here, clearly the evolutionary bias is toward creative evolution, and toward seeing Darwin's impact less in Spencerian terms than as
integrating man with man and with all life in some creative thrust. (One
wonders how much biology enters even into Schopenhauer's avowedly
"metaphysical" argument for the noumenal unity of man, the problem of
seeing personality as "maya" to be penetrated by the initiate). All critics
see "creative evolution" in *The Dynasts*, with its conception of blind Will
gradually becoming conscious; but no one other than Gose has, to my
knowledge, seen the importance of this emphasis in Hardy's *entire* reaction
to Darwin, early and late.

Gose sees Tess as the failure of "psychic evolution" toward some
ultimate form of altruism for all living creatures, a failure that is confirmed
by her murder of Alec. Gose's article is the only piece in Hardy criticism
where the impact of Darwin and the comparative and evolutionary anthropologists (particularly Tylor in *Primitive Culture* [1871] and Frazer in
his early *Totemism* [1887]) is vividly imagined. Hardy was much given to
thinking about evolution in its creative aspect, and to speculating in fictive
ways about the modification of natural evolutionary laws by man's self-
conscious grasp of them and by ethical qualities emerging as "variations."
Most of the Spencerian social analysis according to evolutionary principles
was foreign to Hardy, who apparently took to heart Darwin's admonition
that "in social animals it [natural selection] will adapt the structure of each
individual for the benefit of the community." Still, Hardy's emphasis on the
evolutionary kinship of all creatures rather than on the ruthless struggle for
existence (the Schopenhauerian Will surely resembles some of this latter
view) did not simply produce in him a straightforward desire to imagine
characters in whom this "psychic evolution" toward some ultimate altruism could take place. If Tess's killing the wounded birds is evidence of
some such capacity in her, it also suggests some of the dark implications of
our kinship with all life. Only the reflective, self-conscious mind of man
apparently can sense this evolutionary kinship—yet it is precisely this
capacity that perhaps definitively separates us from other forms of life.

I depart from Elliot Gose when he uses his splendid sense of Hardy's
involvement with the comparative and evolutionary anthropologists to call
Tess a failed psychic evolution. It is no exaggeration to say that Hardy
brooded fictively on the dramatic essence of the "struggle for existence"
and (Spencer's phrase before it was Darwin's) the "survival of the fittest."
Darwin seems to have been as much aware of and concerned about the

metaphoric nature of the word "struggle" as Stanley Edgar Hyman was in his comments on the *The Origin of Species*. The usually quiet drift toward existence or death on the "tangled bank" occasionally becomes, in Hardy, literally a tragic struggle of intrinsically natural man or woman to survive in a world where society has confusingly changed Nature' ambiguous rules of survival. Thus in Tess we have her real affinities with basic natural processes, her limited but important participation in a rudimentary form of ancient folk culture, her introduction to the byways and perversions of "modern" society, especially as Alec manifests them (and as they are symbolically rendered in connection with Alec and the "modern" threshing machine), and finally a betrayal by an imagined denial of modern society in Angel's Hellenistic Nature worship. Significantly, it is really only Angel's lack of any truly Darwinian knowledge of Nature that brings Tess down. Hardy imaginatively but systematically scrutinizes the idea of "survival" and indeed the whole question of who is "fittest" among human beings by subjecting Tess to, as it were, degrees of societal complication and changes in the quality and texture of societal complication. Angel's antisocietal idealism is finally revealed as the most potent corruption of society.

Angel's insistence on Tess's "newness" thus becomes archetypically wrong and destructive for her precisely because Tess is definitively well suited for survival—*provided* that she is not confronted with an actual nemesis. Of course the novel is designed so that she is not spared that confrontation. I do not mean to scientize the novel when I say that it is in a sense a controlled experiment whose outcome is by no means a foregone conclusion for Hardy. Tess's "survival" qualities are, for me, her most essential characteristics. Tough, resilient, healthy, loyal, and persevering, bright enough and yet not too bright, capable of guilt and remorse yet not given to them (so that she can survive in more than a brutish way, in a distinctly human but not at all Christian fashion), a lover with great staying power but no fool and not at all sentimental, Tess is a peculiarly *human* survival ideal—provided we do not finally undercut her entire nature with Christian ideals and Angel's exact perversion of her identification as a natural—a really natural—creature. Some critics have seen Tess as eminently unsuited for survival if she is compared with a Spencerian evolutionary ideal. But "adaptation," as Darwin ambiguously used the word, is a complex set of vibrations between environment and creature and not the ruthless triumph of strength and wiliness, or even of fortitude (understood in a vaguely ethical sense), as Joseph Conrad and Stephen Crane developed the idea in "Falk" or "The Open Boat."

Tess seems to me at least in part Hardy's answer to the following suppositions: Suppose man had not passed beyond heliolatry or the ill-defined folk culture that is not so far removed from its pagan origins in Stonehenge, and that survives in a debased form all around Tess. Suppose he had not been victimized by a Christian *talent* for ideals that generate guilt and remorse and, perhaps even worse, forgiveness as their psychological essence. And suppose, finally, that we are not talking about "survival" solely in a mindless, brutal way (as the d'Urbervilles survived for so long by human measure), but as a quality that both depends on and furthers the peculiar essence of the species; this in man means survival with some sensitivity and awareness of our evolutionary kinship with all life. Who then would be the ideal of survival, as understood in its subtlest Darwinian sense of a symbiosis with the environment that causes the *unique qualities* of this species not only to flourish but to flower, to the point, as Darwin sometimes said, of downright "happiness"? (At rare moments Darwin liked to see this as the outcome of the "struggle.")

Tess is a victim of modern society, but most important she is a victim of Angel's denial of her true, truly Darwinian, affinities with Nature. The geological and paleontological metaphors that Hardy uses firmly establish her ancientness and the ideal quality of her consciousness. She really does come home, then, to Stonehenge —a *pagan*, but as the *ideal* pagan, evolved beyond the paganism of her "noble" and nominally Christian ancestors. She is capable of the "happiness" of a species so attuned to its total environment (Nature and limited forms of society, in her case) that its essence, whatever it may be, flourishes and rejoices. One thinks of the animal poems of Ted Hughes. But Hardy goes beyond Hughes by imagining a fulfillment for man analogous to that possible in other species. Humans in Hughes's poems are always in contrast to the total self-possession (an equality of possession: the self of the environment and the environment of the self) of animals. In his very self-consciousness the human is unnatural, alienated (to repeat the modern clichés) from self itself. Had Tess not been born into a world where the steam-thresher and Alec and Angel dominate, the ideal pagan might at least have gone home to Stonehenge as a genuine sacrifice to the sun, and thus no victim at all.

As Stanley Edgar Hyman has argued, the spiritual impetus of the *Origin* is toward teleology, toward the perfection of species. Even death is rationalized as "a trait evolved by natural selection, permitting a speedier improvement of the higher organisms, and thus an advantage in competition and a good for life." But what is this "perfection" for man? Certainly to Hardy's sensibility it meant what Hyman calls Darwin's ultimate mystery, "a kind of totemic brotherhood, a consubstantiality with all organic beings, resembling St. Paul's 'every one members of one another.' " In his contribution to *Darwin and Modern Science*, Frazer notes that when European first landed on one of the Alaskan islands, the natives took them for a cuttlefish on account of the buttons on their clothes. In a deeper sense, Darwin identifies Europeans as totemic brothers to cuttlefish, and reminds that what he calls in an early notebook " 'animals, our fellow brethren,' are as precious as we in the eyes of our common mother." Manifest in a hundred small and large ways, Tess's great virtue is this sense of evolutionary oneness with life. More significantly, it would also have been her main survival value (as the ecologically minded say it may be ours) and the truly Darwinian "happiness" opens to her except for its defeat by the strategically designed bane of Angel's "naturalism." It is almost as though Hardy were suggesting that this awareness of the evolutionary oneness of all life and perhaps, given Tylor and Frazer, of all culture, is precisely the essence toward which evolution has driven man. Our perfect adaptation depends on this awareness. It is perhaps the only variety of mental awareness that does not isolate man from Nature. To possess it fully would be to become analogous to another creature so perfectly adapted to its environment that its biological "essence" was perfectly expressed. In a sense, humankind would have come home.

In *Tess* the achievement of this Darwinian "perfection" would presumably have meant the fulfillment of her natural sympathy for all creatures, and more importantly a comprehensive evolutionary awareness of her existence —a way of uniting her natural qualities, her folk roots, and the d'Urberville inheritance in an intuitive sense of a large identity "in Nature's teeming family." One of the great mistakes in reading *Tess* is to take her compassion for animals as just another interesting aspect of her character. For one thing, that compassion must somehow be integrated with the fierceness that is equally characteristic of her (if she sympathizes with the wounded birds, equally she breaks their necks). Her sympathy for animals is a sign of the great and extremely subtle Darwinian bias in Hardy's mind when he created her. It must be fitted into her character as it was fitted into Hardy's whole understanding of the evolutionary state of mind and of what Darwin meant by the "perfection" of species and the possible perfection of man.

Thus Hardy's apparently digressive essay when Tess finds herself among the wounded birds is no digression at all:

> She had occasionally caught glimpses of these men in girlhood,
> looking over hedges, or peering through bushes, and pointing
> their guns, strangely accoutred, a bloodthirsty light in their

eyes. She has been told that, rough and brutal as they seemed just then, they were not like this all the year round, but were, in fact, quite civil persons save during certain weeks of autumn and winter, when, like the inhabitants of the Malay Peninsula, they run amuck, and made it their purpose to destroy life — in this case harmless feathered creatures, brought into being by artificial means solely to gratify these propensities — at once so unmannerly and so unchivalrous toward their weaker fellows in Nature's teeming family.

We can hardly read "Nature's teeming family" without seeing in it Hardy's Darwinian emphasis on the relatedness of all creatures. The hunters seem to revert to an earlier, more primitive identity for which they nonetheless *artificially* raise their quarry. The incongruity is genuinely shocking to Hardy. The whole passage is evolutionary not in a Spencerian way but in the way Hardy understood Darwin, and in the way he would have had Tess feel evolution.

Such, and no less, was the vision of Darwin, and the evolutionary, comparative anthropologists pushed to its mystical extremity. I am tempted to believe that in *Tess* Hardy had contemplated its tragic consequences to see if he could imagine it at all. Angel's great sin thus becomes archetypal. In refusing to accept Tess's "experience," in continuing to see her imagined newness irretrievably stained by the seduction, he denies the capacity of Nature to be infinitely old and experienced and yet forever new and virginal. The Darwinian idea of the perfection of the human species demands our sympathy for all truly natural behavior.

Tess: The Making of a Pure Woman

Mary Jacobus

PURITY AND CENSORSHIP

Havelock Ellis, while proclaiming the modernity of Hardy's treatment of sexual questions in *Jude the Obscure*, had an important reservation about *Tess of the D'Urbervilles* (1981):

> I was repelled at the outset by the sub-title. It so happens that I have always regarded the conception of *purity*, when used in moral discussions, as a conception sadly in need of analysis. . . . It seems to me doubtful whether anyone is entitled to use the word "pure" without first defining precisely what he means, and still more doubtful whether an artist is called upon to define it at all, even in several hundred pages. I can quite conceive that the artist should take pleasure in the fact that his own creative revelation of life poured contempt on many old prejudices. But such an effect is neither powerful nor legitimate unless it is engrained in the texture of the narrative; it cannot be stuck on by a label. To me that glaring sub-title meant nothing, and I could not see what it should mean to Mr. Hardy.

The label, Hardy tells us, was added at the last moment, as "the estimate left in a candid mind of the heroine's character" (1912 Preface). It caused trouble from the start. To those who accept a Christian definition of purity,

From *Tearing the Veil: Essays on Femininity.* © 1978 by Routledge & Kegan Paul Ltd. The manuscript of *Tess of the D'Urbervilles* is quoted by permission of the Trustees of the Thomas Hardy Memorial Collection of the British Museum.

it's preposterous; and to those who don't, irrelevant. The difficulty in both cases is the same—that of regarding Tess as somehow immune to the experience she undergoes. To invoke purity in connection with a career that includes not simply seduction, but collapse into kept woman and murderess, taxes the linguistic resources of the most permissive conventional moralist; as the formidable Mrs. Oliphant put it, in a review which epitomises the moral opposition aroused by *Tess*; "here the elaborate and indignant plea for Vice, that it is really Virtue, breaks down altogether." On the other hand, to regard Tess as unimplicated is to deny her the right of participation in her own life. Robbed of responsibility, she is deprived of tragic status—reduced throughout to the victim she does indeed become. Worst of all, she is stripped of the sexual autonomy and the capacity for independent being and doing which are among the most striking features of Hardy's conception.

Hardy himself makes things worse by seeming to adopt the argument for a split between act and intention—Angel Clare comes to realise that "The beauty of a character lay not in its achievements, but in its aims and impulses; the true record lay not among things done, but among things conceived." Yet Angel's response to Tess at the end of the novel is remarkable precisely because he no longer makes this distinction but—knowing her a murderess—accepts her as she is. Alternatively, it could be argued that the terminology of conventional Christian morality is ironically misapplied in order to reveal its inadequacy and challenge the narrow Pauline definition of purity-as-abstinence originally held by Angel. But however one interprets the label, the real problem—as Havelock Ellis points out—is Hardy's failure to "engrain" its implications in the texture of the narrative. In the circumstances, it is illuminating to discover that Tess's purity is a literary construct, "stuck on" in retrospect like the subtitle to meet objections which the novel had encountered even before its publication in 1891. In "Candour in English Fiction," a symposium on the censorship question published in the *New Review* for January 1890, Hardy had protested at the tyranny exercised over the novelist by the conditions of magazine publication. Designed for household reading, the family magazines necessarily failed (in Hardy's words) to "foster the growth of the novel which reflects and reveals life." In particular, a rigid set of taboos—designed to protect "the Young Person" (i.e. the young girl)—governed the fictional treatment of sexual questions. Hardy's experience during the previous months in trying to publish *Tess* lies behind his protest, and the compromises he was about to make must already have been in his mind. Faced with the dilemma of "bring(ing) down the thunders of respectability upon his head" or of "whip(ping) and scourg(ing his) characters into doing something contrary to their natures," he writes of seeing no alternative but to

> do despite to his best imaginative instincts by arranging a dé-
> nouement which he knows to be indescribably unreal and mere-
> tricious, but dear to the Grundyist and subscriber. If the true
> artist ever weeps it probably is then, when he first discovers the
> fearful price that he has to pay for the privilege of writing in the
> English language—no less a price than the complete extinc-
> tion, in the mind of every mature and penetrating reader, of
> sympathetic belief in his personages.

In the autumn of 1889, three successive rejections of the half-completed *Tess* had shown Hardy the price he had to pay, if not for writing in the English language, at any rate for serial publication. Ironically, the very changes he made to placate "the Grundyist and subscriber" produced anomalies which the conventional moralists were quick to seize on when the novel finally appeared.

The form of Hardy's compromise is implicit in his defiant subtitle. But its effects were much more far-reaching. Hardy's own account misleadingly suggests that his solution was a cynical and temporary bowdlerisation for the purposes of serial publication only. In reality he also made lasting modifications to his original conception in an attempt to argue a case whose terms were dictated by the conventional moralists themselves. The attempt profoundly shaped the novel we read today, producing alterations in structure, plot, and characterisation which undermined his fictional argument as well as strengthening it—or rather, since Hardy himself said of *Tess* that "a novel is an impression, not an argument" (1892 Preface), substantially distorted its final impression. As the novel first stood, it was not only simpler in outline, but different in emphasis. A letter to Hardy's American publisher in 1889 merely states that the "personal character and adventures" of his nobly descended milkmaid are "the immediate source of such interest as the tale may have," and notes that "her position is based on fact," but there is no hint of polemic. From the manuscript one can reconstruct the main features of the Ur-*Tess*—already comprising Tess's seduction, the birth and death of her child, Sorrow, and her courtship by Angel, breaking off with their marriage and Angel's wedding-night confession. All the events which make up the second half of the novel (Angel's departure, Tess's solitary ordeal, Alec's reappearance, the murder, and finally the reunion of Tess and Angel before her death) belong to the later, post-1889 phase of composition. More baldly than the revised version, the

Ur-*Tess* had dealt with the common enough situation of a country girl seduced by her employer on first going into service. Her social, economic, and sexual vulnerability are unequivocally defined. Tess's original name, "Love" (modified successively to Cis, Sue, and Rose-Mary before becoming Tess), suggests that Hardy always had in mind the crudely polarised attitudes to female sexuality embodied in Alec d'Urberville and Angel Clare (sexual possession versus idealization). But there is evidence that the oppositions were at this stage less clear-cut, more realistically blurred, and more humanely conceived, than they later became. The original novel was not only less polemical, but elegiacally explored the recurrent Hardian theme implied by its original title, "Too Late, Beloved." This was to be a tragedy of thwarted potential in which unfulfilment expressed not only social and cultural ironies, but the irony of life itself.

Throughout his career Hardy was acutely sensitive to adverse criticism, and the grounds given for its refusal by the three magazines to which *Tess* was offered bear significantly on its reshaping. Hardy had promised the novel to Tillotson's, a newspaper syndicate, but it was only when the portion up to and including the death of Sorrow was already in proof that they read it. Their immediate demand for major changes and deletions led Hardy to try his luck elsewhere. Edward Arnold, the editor of *Murray's Magazine*, wrote a friendly, regretful, but firm refusal based on his decision not to publish what he called "stories where the plot involves frequent and detailed reference to immoral situations." Arnold explicitly takes his stand on the opposite side of a contemporary debate to which Hardy himself was to contribute in another *New Review* symposium, "The Tree of Knowledge" (1894), this time about sex education for women:

> I know well enough (writes Arnold) that these tragedies are being played out every day in our midst, but I believe the less publicity they have the better, and that it is quite possible and very desirable for women to grow up and pass through life without the knowledge of them.

In this version of the double standard, middle- and upper-class women are to be sheltered from knowing what men of the same class get up to with working-class women. But is was the third and last rejection of *Tess* that proved most decisive for its development. It must also have been most wounding, based as it was not on an objection of principle, but on specific objections to Hardy's treatment of his subject. Mowbray Morris, the editor of *Macmillan's Magazine*—later to reply to "Candour in English Fiction " with an editorial of his own—reacted sharply to the frankness with which Hardy had made Tess's seduction the central feature of his novel:

> It is obvious from the first page what is to be Tess's fate at Trantridge; it is apparently obvious also to the mother, who does not seem to mind, consoling herself with the somewhat cynical reflection that she may be made a lady *after* if not *before*. All the first part therefore is a sort of prologue to the girl's seduction which is hardly ever, and can hardly ever be out of the reader's mind.

He goes on to reveal particular unease about the prominence given to Tess's sexuality, both in its own right and in its effect on others:

> Even Angel Clare (he complains) . . . has not as yet got beyond a purely sensuous admiration for her person. Tess herself does not appear to have any feelings of this sort about her; but her capacity for stirring and by implication for gratifying these feelings for others is pressed rather more frequently and elaborately than strikes me as altogether convenient. . . . You use the word *succulent* more than once to describe the general appearance and condition of the Frome Valley. Perhaps I might say that the general impression left on me by reading your story . . . is one of rather too much succulence.

Morris's prejudices—against women capable of sexual arousal as well as of arousing others—are revealing in themselves; in an anonymous and hostile review of the novel as it finally appeared, he was again to accuse Hardy of tastelessly parading what he calls his heroine's "sensual qualifications for the part." It is in the light of such reactions that Hardy's purification of Tess must be seen. The changes he made tell us not only about the strains which underlie one of his greatest novels, but about late Victorian attitudes to female sexuality.

REHABILITATION

Hardy's reply to Arnold is summed up in the words of the "Explanatory Note" to the first edition: "If an offence come out of the truth, better is it that the offence come than that the truth be concealed." His reply to Morris is contained in his subtitle. A sustained campaign of rehabilitation makes Tess's so blatant a case of the double standard of sexual morality applied to men and women, and Tess herself so blameless, that the tragedy of the ordinary becomes the tragedy of the exceptional—blackening both man and fate in the process. In Hardy's original scheme, Tess becomes exceptional precisely through the experience she undergoes. She starts as a village girl distinguished from others only by her freshness, her ancestry, and the fecklessness of her parents. The gap between herself and her mother seems less great and, importantly, she has known of her pedigree "ever since her infancy." In the revised version, however, "Sir John" first learns of his lineage in the opening scene of the book. Hardy's intention in making this change is obviously to play down the inevitability of which Morris complained. Originally, her seduction had sprung from a realistic combination of circumstances—her mother's simple-mindedness (seeing Alec's attentions as Tess's chance to marry a gentleman), her father's irresponsibility (getting too drunk to drive the loaded cart to market, and hence throwing on Tess the guilt of Prince's death), and her own inexperience. In the revised manuscript, her entire tragedy springs from this opening encounter with an antiquarian parson, and can now be blamed on a peculiarly malign chain of events. With this development of the heroine's ancestry into the mainspring of her tragedy goes the endowing of Tess herself with special qualities of dignity and refinement. Mrs. Oliphant calls it "a pardonable extravagance" in a partisan author to make her "a kind of princess" in her village milieu. But is it? Later in the novel, Angel Clare recognises that the consciousness on which he has intruded is Tess's single opportunity of existence—that she is "a woman, who at her lowest estimate as an ordinary mortal had a life which, to herself who endured or enjoyed it, possessed as great a dimension and importance as the life of the mightiest to him." Though we see Tess as one anonymous field-woman among others, harvesting at Marlott or turnip-hacking at Flintcomb-Ash, her inner world is unique. To make her tragedy inseparable from her distinction is to belie the humane and egalitarian impulse at the heart of the novel—its assertion of the value of any individual, however commonplace, however obscure.

To give Tess from the start a privileged sensibility—make her especially conscious of her parents' shortcomings, especially responsible, especially alert to the implications of Alec's behaviour—also works against a central motif in the Ur-*Tess*: that of growth through experience. Hardy's conception of character is an organic one. He starts with an unformed heroine, and shows us the emergence of a reflective consciousness close to his own. Tess's "corporeal blight had been her mental harvest," he observes; the seduction and its aftermath leave her with a sombre sense of personal insignificance and vulnerability. In her own language she expresses what Hardy calls "the spirit of modernism." the uncertainty of life without a benign providence or an assured future:

> you see numbers of to-morrows just all in a line, the first of them the biggest and clearest, the others getting smaller and smaller as they stand further away; but they all seem very fierce and cruel, and as if they said, "Beware o' me! Beware o' me!"

In this respect, *Tess*—like so many of Hardy's novels—concerns education. The actuality and the metaphor of journeying pervade the novel, reflecting both Tess's changing circumstances, and, most movingly, her capacity for endurance. In a particularly interesting passage Hardy extends the metaphor to embrace education through experience, drawing on a quotation from Ascham's *Schoolmaster*: " 'By experience,' " says Roger Ascham, " 'we find out a short way by a long wandering.' " Not seldom that long wandering unfits us for further travel, and of what use is our experience to us then?" The context of Ascham's remark had been a criticism of experience as a mode of teaching:

> Learning teacheth more in one year than experience in twenty, and learning teacheth safely, when experience maketh more miserable than wise. He hazardeth sore that waxeth wise by experience . . . We know by experience itself that it is a marvelous pain to find out but a short way by long wandering.

Wise fathers, he continues, teach their children rather than committing them to the school of life—an injunction picked up when Tess turns on her mother with the lament, " 'Why didn't you tell me there was danger? Why didn't you warn me?' "

A necessary consequence of Hardy's campaign to purify Tess is the character-assassination of Alec and Angel. Hardy's remark that, "but for the world's opinion," her seduction would have been counted "rather a liberal education to her than otherwise" was always sweeping in view of its result, Sorrow. But it makes more sense in the context of the relationship with Alec as originally envisaged. At this stage Alec had been younger (21 or 22 rather than 23 or 24) and without the later element of fraud. Instead of being a spurious d'Urberville, a nouveau-riche with a stolen name, he is simply a yeoman-farmer called Hawnferne. Traces of this less hardened character live on in the episode—not present, of course, in the original version— in which Tess goes to claim kin at the Slopes and first meets Alec. We are told that "a sooty fur represented for the present the dense black moustache that was to be" (by the first edition, in 1891, it has grown to "a well-groomed black moustache with curled points"); although in training for the role, he is not yet the moustachioed seducer of Victorian melodrama. Present from the start, however, is the motif of sexual dominance expressed through mechanical power. In the opening pages of the Ur-*Tess*, Alec has seen Tess at the club-walking and called on her mother; as she drives along in the small hours of the next morning, Tess's last thoughts before dropping off and waking to find Prince impaled by the on-coming mail-coach are of the young man "whose gig was part of his body." Alec's gig—here tellingly juxtaposed with the death of Prince —is not simply the equivalent of a sports car, his badge of machismo, wealth and social status. It is also a symbolic expression of the way in which Tess is to be deprived of control over her own body, whether by Alec himself or by the alien rhythms of the threshing machine at Flintcomb-Ash, in a scene where sexual and economic oppression are as closely identified as they had been in her seduction.

The gig motif makes the nature of Alec's power over Tess particularly explicit. But it also provides scope for the rough and tumble of a more robustly-conceived situation in their two most important scenes together, the drive to the Slopes and—in the Ur-*Tess*—the night of the seduction itself. It is in these scenes that the effect of Hardy's later modifications to the character of Tess emerges most clearly. The drive to the Slopes, Tess's first real encounter with Alec, shows her confused but sturdy in the face of his sexual bullying; above all, it shows her as less conscious. After being forced to clasp his waist during one of the pell-mell downhill gallops contrived by Alec for the purpose, the original Tess exclaims " 'Safe thank God!' . . . *with a sigh of relief*"; the later, more aware Tess adds " 'in spite of your folly!' . . . *her face on fire.*" In the same way, after her ruse to get out of the gig (letting her hat blow off), she refuses to get up again with " 'No Sir,' she said, *firmly and smiling*"—whereas the later, more sophisticated Tess reveals "the red and ivory of her mouth *in defiant triumph.*" The original relationship is thus both more straightforward and more intimate. Just before the seduction itself, Hardy comments in the manuscript version that "a familiarity with his presence, which (Alec) had carefully cultivated in (Tess) had removed all her original shyness of him"; and we see this familiarity in the earlier version of the scene in which Alec gives her a whistling lesson. Tess purses her lips as he instructs, "laughing however" (revised to "laughing *distressfully* however," and when she produces a note "the momentary pleasure of success got the better of her; and she involuntarily smiled in his face *like a child*"—the last phrase deleted from the revised version. This more naïve and trusting Tess figures in the prelude to her seduction, the orgiastic Trantridge dance. As she looks on, waiting for company on her homeward walk, Alec appears; and we see her confiding her problem to him, declining his offer of a lift warily ("'I am much obliged to 'ee, sir,' she answered") but without the formality of the later version—"'I am much obliged,' she answered frigidly"—where she has become the alert repulser of his attentions. The suggestion of greater intimacy is picked up in a conversation later that night, after Alec has rescued Tess from the Amazonian sisters who pick a quarrel with her on the way home:

> "(Tess), how many times have I kissed you since you have been here?"
> "You know as well as I."
> "Not many."
> "Too many."
> "Only about four times, and never once on the lips, because you turn away so."

This is inconveniently explicit in the context of a purified Tess, and it is deleted altogether from the later version. But it reflects the greater degree of intimacy permitted by the Ur-*Tess*, which in turn makes the seduction itself credible.

"The girl who escapes from her fellow-servants in their jollity by jumping up on horseback . . . behind a master of such a character, and being carried off by him in the middle of the night, naturally leaves her reputation behind her." Mrs. Oliphant's absurd verdict is unexpectedly pertinent to the revised version. But the problem doesn't arise in the Ur-*Tess*. Once again the gig—the more prosaic but more probable means of Tess's rescue in the original version—plays an important part in this crucial scene. In the later version, Tess reacts to Alec's attempt to put his arm round her by a little push that threatens to make him lose his balance, perched sideways on his horse with her behind him. In the Ur-*Tess*, however, she reacts with an unladylike vigour which makes him fall right out of the gig and onto the ground, winding him in the process. Alec makes the most of his fall, capitalising on her genuine alarm and penitence—"'O I am so sorry, Mr. Hawnferne! Have I hurt you? Have I killed 'ee? Do speak to me!'"—to renew his complaints about being kept at arm's length. The incident puts Tess firmly in the wrong, and makes her acquiesce in driving on beside him with his arm round her ("'because I thought I had wronged you by that push,'" until she realises that they are nowhere near home. It is at this point that Hardy introduces the motif of intoxication which printed versions omit after 1891. Earlier, the death of Prince had been the direct result of her father's drunkenness and Tess's exhaustion. Hawnferne's is specifically described as a drinking farm, and the Trantridge dance, with its stupefied couples falling to the ground, prepares for Tess's own collapse in the Chase. She too is caught up in the Trantridge ethos when she accepts Alec's offer of a warming draught of spirits before he goes off to look for the road. The logic of the scenario—confused, realistically mingling accident and design, character and situation—is entirely convincing. When Tess looks back on the events leading up to her fall, she reflects accurately enough: "She had never cared for him, she did not care for him now. She had dreaded him, winced at him, succumbed to him, and that was all." In 1892 Hardy accentuated Alec's role as seducer by adding "succumbed *to a cruel advantage he took of her helplessness.*" But it needed more than this to transform seduction into the near-rape demanded by the purification of Tess, and at the same time Hardy added the comments of the Marlott villagers as Tess suckles her child in the harvest-field:

> A little more than persuading had to do wi' the coming o't....
> There were they that heard a sobbing one night last year in The Chase; and it mid ha' gone hard wi' a certain party if folks had come along.

Like Milton, Hardy has produced two versions of the fall—one, comprehensible in human terms, the other retrospectively imposed for the sake of his argument.

THE WAGES OF SIN

The aftermath of Tess's stay at the Slopes is explicitly postlapsarian; Tess has discovered that "the serpent hisses where the sweet birds sing," and she makes her exit from the paradise of unknowing pursued by the text-painter's flaming letters: "THE, WAGES, OF, SIN, IS, DEATH" (in the first edition, "THY, DAMNATION, SLUMBERETH, NOT"). Manuscript evidence suggests that the period of Tess's dejection at Marlott originally occupied a larger space, which encourages the idea that Hardy had wished to stress its part in bringing the mature Tess into being. Paradoxically, it is her seduction that has made her a fitting counterpart to the high-minded Angel Clare:

> At a leap almost [Tess] changed from simple girl to dignified woman. Symbols of reflectiveness passed into her face, and a

> note of tragedy at times into her voice. Her eyes grew larger
> and more eloquent. She became what would have been called a
> fine creature . . . a woman whom the turbulent experiences of
> the last year or two had quite failed to demoralize.

Angel has been reflective by thought as she has been by life — talking the language of religious disaffection where she expresses her sense of dissonance in the language of experience (" 'there are always more ladies than lords when you come to peel 'em' "). Angel's dissent from the rigid fundamental Christianity of his father, together with his harp-playing, single him out at once as a thinking and a feeling man. The congruence of their sensibilities is beautifully evoked in the overgrown garden where Tess has been listening to Angel's playing. The garden perfectly expresses the erotic potential of their relationship — potential coloured by the implications of a fallen world. As she "undulate[s] upon [Angel's] notes as upon billows," Tess is surrounded by a strange-smelling wilderness, "damp and rank with succulent grass and tall blooming weeds," in which snails climb the stems of apple trees and sticky blights make blood-red stains on Tess's skin. Melancholy and sensuousness are fused in the highly-charged atmosphere of a June evening: "The floating pollen seemed to be his notes made visible, and the dampness of the garden the tears of its sensibility." The same blend of sensibility with the "succulence" complained of by Morris (dutifully revised to "juicy") characterises their scenes of courtship in the richly fertile Frome valley — scenes to which Hardy once again made significant modifications.

Just as the purification of Tess had demanded the blackening of Alec, it also required an increase in Angel's coldness and, as before, in Tess's reticence. Like Alec, the original Angel had been a younger and more believable character—bowled over by Tess, perhaps against his better judgment, having had no thoughts of marriage before. The early scenes between them are pervaded by mutual sexual attraction which small but significant revisions attempt to play down. For instance, when Tess archly accuses Angel of ranging the cows to her advantage, her smile "lifted her upper lip gently in the middle so as to show three or four of her teeth, while the lower remained still;" "*severely* still" is the correction. Angel, burdened in one manuscript reading by a "*growing madness* of passion . . . for the *seductive* Tess" is less overwhelmed in the final version by a "waxing fervour of passion" for a chastely "soft and silent" Tess. The crystallising moment for both, their first embrace, is similarly censored. When Angel comes impulsively round behind the cow Tess is milking and takes her in his arms, the first version reads: "[Tess] yielded to Angel's embrace as unreflectingly as a child. Having seen that it was really her lover and no one else, her lips parted, she panted in her impressionability, and burst into a succession of ecstatic sobs." In the later version, Tess is more restrained: "her lips parted, and she sank upon him in her momentary joy, *with something very like an ecstatic cry*." Angel has been on the point of "*violently kissing*" Tess's mouth, and declares himself "*passionately* devoted" to her; we lose both the violence and the passion, while Tess's emotion merely leads her to "become agitated" where before she had begun "to sob in reality." As Angel "burns" to be with her, so Tess is permitted to be fully responsive; equally disturbed by their embrace, the two of them (not just the Angel of the later version) keep apart — "palpitating bundles of nerves as both of them were." In so far as they are distinguished at this stage, it is by a love that is intellectual and imaginative on his side, and full of "impassioned warmth" on hers. Angel is conceived, in contrast to Alec, as a man in whom imagination and conscience are inseparable from love; he wins Tess's "tender respect" precisely by his restraint, and we are told that though he "could love intensely . . . his love was more specifically of the solicitous and cherishing mood" by 1891 it is a love "inclined to the imaginative and ethereal"). Only in the post-1889 section of the novel do we hear of a love "ethereal to a fault, imaginative to impracticability," of Angel's "will to subdue his physical emotion to his ideal emotion" and "his small compressed mouth."

The Angel of the Ur-*Tess* is scrupulous rather than obsessional. Hardy has created an altogether more pitying portrait of a man who cannot cope with the implications of the sexuality to which he none the less responds — unconsciously preferring Tess spiritualised by the light of dawn. Although he warms to the instinctual, easy-going life of the dairy, he retains the morality of the vicarage. As Alec is trapped by his own code of seduction and betrayal, so Angel was to have been trapped by his puritan upbringing. We are told that "despite his heterodox opinions" (changed in 1892 to "heterodoxy, faults, and weaknesses," Angel never envisages sex outside marriage. His acceptance of the ethical code practised by his parents, despite his rejection of what he calls "the miraculous" element in Christianity, was to have been central to his tragedy. It is in Angel's confession that Hardy's falsification of his original intention can be seen most clearly. Angel's religious dissent has been crucial, not only in preventing his entering the Church like his brothers, but in preventing his going to university. No less than Tess, he is socially displaced, and, in the eyes of his family at least, damned for his views. The confession which he embarks on in the Ur-*Tess* is quite simply one of unbelief:

"Tess, have you noticed that though I am a parson's son, I don't go to church?"

"I have — occasionally."

"Did you ever think why?"

"I thought you did not like the parson of the parish."

"It was not that, for I don't know him. Didn't it strike you as strange that being so mixed up with the church by family ties and traditions I have not entered it but have done the odd thing of learning to be a farmer?"

"It did once or twice, dear Angel."

That the subject is clearly of more importance to Angel than Tess accentuates the intellectual gap between them. We cannot know how Angel would have continued, since at this point in the manuscript two pages have been condensed into one. A pencil draft for the final version, on the back of the surviving leaf, could suggest that Hardy had originally occupied the missing page with a much fuller statement of Angel's ethical position in the form of an extended quotation from St Paul (including an explicit denunciation of "chambering and wantonness" as well as the more general injunction preserved in the final version: " 'Be thou an example — in word, in conversation, in charity, in spirit, in faith, in purity' " (1 Timothy 4:12). What is lacking is any indication whether Hardy had intended Angel to confess to a sexual episode in his own past paralleling Tess's. But although the Ur-*Tess* is disappointingly incomplete here, the clinching piece of evidence is provided by Hardy's earlier reference to this brief affair with an older woman, since it occurs on a new half page pasted to an old one, onto which extra material has clearly been fitted. The only reason for so substantial a revision would have been to make this earlier account of Angel's career square with a crucial change in his confession — a change motivated by Hardy's need to present a black and white case for Tess.

If Alec becomes an implausible villain, Angel, with his talk of purity, becomes a hypocritical proponent of the double standard. The overstatement does more than strain credibility — it falsifies Hardy's humane vision of individuals trapped by themselves and the ironies of their past. "Too Late, Beloved" takes on new force in the light of Tess's marriage to the man least able to overlook her deviation from Pauline ethics. That the virginal milkmaid of Angel's imagination is no longer "pure" is as tragic for him as for her in the Ur-*Tess*. Significantly, it is only on their wedding night in the original version that Angel learns of the decayed aristocratic descent to which he has slightingly referred on previous occasions (his unexpected pride in Tess's ancestry is an invention of the later version, where she confesses to it at an earlier stage). Theirs had been tragedy of mutual incomprehension, almost, a collision of cultures as well as morals. The gulf between them is nowhere clearer than in Tess's original pre-paredness, before their marriage, to accept "another kind of union with him, for his own sake, had he urged it upon her; that he might have re-treated if discontented with her on learning her story." Though less easy-going than her mother, Tess had been able to envisage an alternative to Angel's scrupulous morality. But such a thought is not allowed to cross the mind of a purified Tess; instead, the later version encumbers her with the naïve and exonerating belief—displayed only after the confession (i.e., in the post-1889 phase of composition)—that Angel could divorce her if he wished. This high-minded heroine is not the same as the Tess of earlier scenes, torn between her desire to be honest with Angel and an under-standable longing for happiness at all costs. With purification comes in-authenticity and a new straining for effect in a novel previously marked by its realism. Angel's rigidity, Tess's humility, are equally forced; and it is surely significant that in the scenes immediately following the confession —that is, in the first scenes to be written when the novel was resumed after its successive rejections—Hardy's imagination should be seen to be labouring under precisely the adverse conditions described by "Candour in English Fiction."

Aftermath

It would be wrong to imply that everything belonging to the later, post-1889 phase of composition fell short of an earlier truth to life. Tess's desolate period at Flintcomb-Ash is enough to show Hardy's imagination functioning at its best, creating a universal predicament out of individuals at work in a hostile landscape which at once mirrors and dwarfs their suffering. All the same, Hardy continued to modify his narrative even beyond this stage. Traces of his original conception linger on especially in his handling of Alec, whose reappearance initiates the final movement of the novel. Predictably, Hardy superimposes the portrait of a fully formed rake on the Alec of the Trantridge period ("the aforetimed curves of sen-suousness," "the lip-shapings that had meant seductiveness," "the bold prominent eye that had flashed upon her shrinking form in the old time with such heartless and cruel grossness"). But the sincerity of Alec's con-version, and the genuine agony of his loss of faith, are not questioned in the manuscript. There is irony and factitiousness, but not hedonism or fraud.

The Alec who can say of his new-found faith, " 'If you could only know, Tess, the sense of security, the certainty that you can never fall away . . .' " is expressing a religious sense deliberately dissipated by the text of 1902: " 'If you could only know, Tess, *the pleasure of having a good slap at yourself.*' " Tess's angry outburst first meets with " 'Tess . . . don't speak so. It came to me like a shining light;' " only in 1902, again, does this become " 'It came to me *like a jolly new idea.*' " When Alec reproaches himself for " 'the whole blackness of the sin, the awful, awful iniquity' " (emended in 1902 to " '*the whole unconventional business of our time at Trantridge,*' " we may recoil from the crude language of Christian condemnation, but it does not seem cynical. The impression is of a man, however mistakenly, attempting to right an old wrong in the terms laid down by his new morality, and made wretched by the reawakening of sexual passion—coming to see Tess with a marriage license in his pocket, visiting her later when he should be preaching to the "poor sinners" (by 1902, "*poor drunken boobies,*") who await him elsewhere, and leaving her with the words, " 'I'll go away—to hide—and—ah, can I!—pray' " (secularised in 1902 to " 'I'll go away—*to swear*—and—ah, can I! *mend*' "). Angel's had been an intellectual tragedy: Alec's, a tragedy of passion. Ironically, it is Angel's arguments, retailed by Tess, which lead Alec to lose the faith to which he had been converted by Angel's father and which pave the way back to Tess. Here Hardy's target is less Alec himself than the religious doctrine which once more injures Tess in its failure to encompass the heterodoxy of human experience.

Mrs. Oliphant wrote indignantly of Tess's collapse, "If Tess did this, then Tess . . . was at twenty a much inferior creature to the unawakened Tess at sixteen who would not live upon the wages of iniquity." Exactly; Tess's suffering may deepen her, but it breaks her in the end. If the wages of sin is death, the wages of virtue—as we see at Flintcomb-Ash—are grinding poverty and back-breaking labour. As Tess puts it succinctly when Angel finds her living with Alec at Sandbourne, " 'He bought me' " (by 1891, more reticently, " 'He———' "). Hardy's imaginative allegiance to Tess does not flinch from her subsequent act of murder—carried out with triumphant thoroughness in the earliest manuscript readings. The workman who finds Alec's body reports graphically " 'He has been stabbed—*the carving knife is sticking up in his heart*' " (toned down to " 'He has been hurt with the carving knife' "), and Hardy himself underlines Tess's violence with "The knife had been *driven through the heart* of the victim" (similarly toned down to "The wound was small, but the point of the knife had touched the heart of the victim"). Later, when Tess tells Angel of the murder, she does so with "a *triumphant* smile" not "a pitiful white smile";

" 'I have done it *well*,' " she claims, rather than the conventionally helpless " 'I have done it—I don't know how.' " Hardy perhaps wished to play down Tess's unbalance for the sake of propriety, but his initial response to this imagined act is surely ours—that it repays the injustice to which Tess has been subjected throughout the book. Here, as elsewhere, Hardy's intuitive commitment was incompletely suppressed by the terms of reference imposed on him. Tess is not a woman to be admired for her purity or condemned for the lack of it; simply, she is a human being whose right to be is affirmed on every page, and whose death is the culminating injustice.

Mowbray Morris—to whom *Tess* was "a coarse and disagreeable story (told) in a coarse and disagreeable manner"—summed up the proper purpose of fiction in his editorial reply to "Candour in English Fiction": "to console, to refresh, to amuse; to lighten the heavy and the weary weight, not to add to it; to distract, not to disturb." Hardy's own very different views were incorporated into the novel itself in the cancelled paragraph which originally introduced his final chapter and the hanging of Tess:

> The humble delineator of human character and human contingencies, whether his narrative deal with the actual or with the typical only, must primarily and above all things be sincere, however terrible sincerity may be. Gladly sometimes would such an one lie, for dear civility's sake, but for the ever-haunting afterthought, "This work was not honest, and may do harm." In typical history with all its liberty, there are, as in real history, features which can never be distorted with impunity and issues which should never be falsified. And perhaps in glancing at the misfortunes of such people as have or could have lived we may acquire some art in shielding from like misfortunes those who have yet to be born. If truth requires justification, surely this is an ample one.

The question must be asked: did Hardy lie, if only "for dear civility's sake?" Surely not. Though he chose to compromise in order to make his case and gain a hearing, he never falsified the issues. For all its blackening and whitewashing, the final version of *Tess of the D'Urbervilles* is justified not only by its power to move and disturb, but by its essential truth.

Tess of the D'Urbervilles: Repetition as Immanent Design

J. Hillis Miller

The narrative fabric of *Tess of the D'Urbervilles* is woven of manifold repetitions—verbal, thematic, and narrative. At the same time, it is a story about repetition. This might be expressed by saying that the story of Tess poses a question: Why is it that Tess is "destined" to live a life which both exists in itself as the repetition of the same event in different forms and at the same time repeats the previous experience of others in history and in legend? What compels her to repeat both her own earlier life and the lives of others? What compels her to become a model which will be repeated later by others? The question on the methodological level might be phrased by asking not why literary works tend to contain various forms of repetition, which goes without saying, but what concept of repetition, in this particular case, will allow the reader to understand the way the repetitions work here to generate meaning. Another way to put this question is to ask what, for *Tess of the D'Urbervilles*, is the appropriate concept of difference. Are the differences between one example of a motif and another in a given case accidental or essential?

I shall concentrate on the interpretation of a single important passage in the novel, the one describing Alec's violation of Tess. This passage is one in which many forms of repetition are both operative and overtly named. I have called what happens to Tess her "violation." To call it either a rape or

From *Fiction and Repetition: Seven English Novels.* © 1982 by J. Hillis Miller. Harvard University Press, 1982. A few words from the original manuscript of *Tess of the D'Urbervilles* that differ from the published versions appear in this essay. Excerpts from the manuscript are printed by permission of the Trustees of the late Miss E. A. Dugdale.

a seduction would beg the fundamental questions which the book raises, the questions of the meaning of Tess's experience and of its causes. Here is the passage:

> D'Urberville stooped; and heard a gentle regular breathing. He knelt and bent lower, till her breath warmed his face, and in a moment his cheek was in contact with hers. She was sleeping soundly, and upon her eyelashes there lingered tears.
>
> Darkness and silence ruled everywhere around. Above them rose the primeval yews and oaks of The Chase, in which were poised gentle roosting birds in their last nap; and about them stole the hopping rabbits and hares. But, might some say, where was Tess's guardian angel? where was the providence of her simple faith? Perhaps, like that other god of whom the ironical Tishbite spoke, he was talking, or he was pursuing, or he was in journey, or he was sleeping and not to be awaked.
>
> Why it was that upon this beautiful feminine tissue, sensitive as gossamer, and practically blank as snow as yet, there should have been traced such a coarse pattern as it was doomed to receive; why so often the coarse appropriates the finer thus, the wrong man the woman, the wrong woman the man, many thousand years of analytical philosophy have failed to explain to our sense of order. One may, indeed, admit the possibility of a retribution lurking in the present catastrophe. Doubtless some of Tess d'Urberville's mailed ancestors rollicking home from a fray had dealt the same measure even more ruthlessly toward peasant girls of their time. But though to visit the sins of the fathers upon their children may be a morality good enough for divinities, it is scorned by average human nature; and it therefore does not mend the matter.
>
> As Tess's own people down in those retreats are never tired of saying among each other in their fatalistic way: "It was to be." There lay the pity of it. An immeasurable social chasm was to divide our heroine's personality there-after from that previous self of hers who stepped from her mother's door to try her fortune at Trantridge poultry-farm.

I have said that this passage describes Tess's violation. Yet, as almost all commentators on the scene have noted, the event is in fact not described at all, or at any rate it is not described directly. It exists in the text only as a blank space, like Tess's "beautiful feminine tissue . . . practically blank as snow as yet." It exists in the gap between paragraphs in which the event has not yet occurred and those which see it as already part of the irrevocable past. It exists in the novel as a metaphor. Doubtless Hardy was not free to describe such a scene literally. The reader will remember in this connection the notorious fact that in the first periodical version of *Tess*, in *The Graphic*, Hardy had to have Angel Clare wheel Tess and the other girls across a puddle in a wheel-barrow rather than carry them across in his arms. The episode of Tess's violation by Alec does not occur in *The Graphic* version at all. Even so, the effacement of the actual moment of Tess's loss of virginity, its vanishing from the text of the finished novel, is significant and functional. It is matched by the similar failure to describe directly all the crucial acts of violence which echo Tess's violation before and after its occurrence: the killing of the horse, Prince, when Tess falls asleep at the reins, the murder of Alec, the execution of Tess. Death and sexuality are two fundamental human realities, events which it seems ought to be present or actual when they happen, if any events are present and actual. In *Tess* they happen only offstage, beyond the margin of the narration, as they do in Greek tragedy. They exist in the novel in displaced expressions, like that gigantic ace of hearts on the ceiling which is the sign that Alec has been murdered, or like the distant raising of the black flag which is the sign that Tess has been hanged.

The sign in the novel of Tess's violation, the metaphor which is its indirect presence in Hardy's language, has a deeper significance than those of the more straightforward ace of hearts or black flag. Tess's rape or seduction exists in the novel in a metaphor of drawing. It is the marking out of a pattern on Tess's flesh. "Analytical philosophy," says the narrator, cannot explain "why it was that upon this beautiful feminine tissue . . . there should have been traced such a coarse pattern as it was doomed to receive." This metaphor belongs to a chain of figures of speech in the novel, a chain that includes the tracing of a pattern, the making of a mark, the carving of a line or sign, and the act of writing.

Writing and the making of a trace are also associated in the poem, "Tess's Lament." The poem, like the prefaces and the subtitle, says the novel again in a different way. Tess says in the poem:

> I cannot bear my fate as writ,
> I'd have my life unbe;
> Would turn my memory to a blot,
> Make every relic of me rot,
> My doings be as they were not,
> And gone all trace of me!

All the elements in this chain of metaphors in one way or another involve a physical act which changes a material substance, marking it or inscribing something on it. It then becomes no longer simply itself but the sign of something absent, something which has already happened. It becomes a "relic" or a "trace."

Hardy's feelings about Tess were strong, perhaps stronger than for any other of his invented personages. He even obscurely identified himself with her. The reader here encounters an example of that strange phenomenon in which a male author invents a female protagonist and then falls in love with her, so to speak, pities her, suffers with her, takes her to his bosom, as Hardy's epigraph from *Two Gentlemen of Verona* affirms he did in the case of Tess: "Poor wounded name, my bosom as a bed/Shall lodge thee." Trollope's feelings about Lily Dale in *The Small House at Allington* and in *The Last Chronicle of Barset* are another example of this. No good reader of *Tess of the D'Urbervilles* can fail, in his or her turn, to be deeply moved by the novel or by the poem cited above. I for one find the description of Angel Clare's failure to consummate his marriage to Tess almost unbearably painful. The emotional experience of following through the novel no doubt forms that background of agreement about the novel which is shared by almost all readers and forms the basis for discussions of it and even for disagreements about what the novel means. This might be compared to Roman Jakobson's persuasive argument that though theorists of prosody may endlessly disagree about the metrical form of a given set of verses, nevertheless the lines "have" a rhythm which is experienced, at least in some form, by any competent reader. It is because all good readers of *Tess* would agree that Tess suffers and even tend to agree that she does not wholly deserve her suffering, and it is because all good readers of *Tess* share in the narrator's sympathy and pity for that suffering, that we care about the question of why Tess suffers so. At the same time, apparently casual, peripheral, or "abstract" elements, such as the use of the figure of writing to describe Tess's deflowering, are not foreign to her suffering or to the reader's re-experience of it. The figures are a major vehicle for the communication of the emotional rhythms the novel and its adjacent poem create in the reader. What could be more moving than to know that Tess's self-hatred or self-disparagement is so great that, thinking of her life as having made an ugly inscription on the world, like a shocking graffito on a wall, she wants every "trace" of herself obliterated. Because the reader is moved, he may want to understand just what is implied by Hardy's repeated use of this metaphor.

The metaphor of the tracing of a pattern has a multiple significance.

It assimilates the real event to the act of writing about it. It defines both the novel and the events it presents as repetitions, as the outlining again of a pattern which already somewhere exists. Tess's violation exists, both when it "first" happens and in the narrator's telling, as the re-enactment of an event which has already occurred. The physical act itself is the making of a mark, the outlining of a sign. This deprives the event of any purely present existence and makes it a design referring backward and forward to a long chain of similar events throughout history. Tess's violation repeats the violence her mailed ancestors did to the peasant girls of their time. In another place in the novel, Tess tells Angel Clare she does not want to learn about history, and gives expression to a vision of time as a repetitive series. Tess does not want to know history because, as she says, "what's the use of learning that I am one of a long row only—finding out that there is set down in some old book somebody just like me, and to know that I shall only act her part; making me sad, that's all. The best is not to remember that your nature and your past doings have been like thousands' and thousands', and that your coming life and doings'll be like thousands' and thousands'" (ch.19).

Sex, physical violence, and writing all involve a paradoxical act of cutting, piercing, or in some way altering some physical object. The paradox lies in the fact that the fissure at the same time establishes a continuity. It makes the thing marked a repetition and gives it in one way or another the power of reproducing itself in the future. The word "paradox," in fact, is not, strictly speaking, appropriate here, since it presupposes a prior logical coherence which the paradox violates, going against what is normally taught or said. The dividing fissure which at the same time joins, in this case, is prior to logic, in the sense, for example, of the logical coherence of a plot with beginning, middle, and end. Any example of the division which joins is already a repetition, however far back one goes to seek the first one. This chapter attempts to identify this alogic or this alternative logic of plot and to justify giving it the Hardyan name of repetition as *immanent* design. Such a plot will be without beginning and end in the Aristotelian sense, and the elements in the "middle" will not be organized according to determined causal sequence. The acts of sexual conjunction, of physical violence, and of writing create gaps or breaks, as, for example, "an immeasurable social chasm was to divide our heroine's personality thereafter from that previous self of hers."

All three of these acts in *Tess* converge in the multiple implications of the metaphor of grafting used to describe the relation of Tess and Alec. The metaphor is overt when the narrator says that though the spurious

Stoke-d'Urbervilles were not "of the true tree," nevertheless, "this family formed a very good stock whereon to regraft a name which sadly wanted such renovation" (ch. 5), or when Tess's father says of Alec, "sure enough he mid have serious thoughts about improving his blood by linking on to the old line" (ch. 6), or when her mother says, "as one of the genuine stock, she ought to make her way with 'en, if she plays her trump card aright" (ch. 7). The metaphor of grafting may be present covertly, according to a characteristically complex conjunction of motifs, when the rapid ride Tess takes with Alec in the dog cart, the ride that leads to Alec giving her "the kiss of mastery" (ch. 8), is described in the metaphor of a splitting stick: "The aspect of the straight road enlarged with their advance, the two banks dividing like a splitting stick; one rushing past at each shoulder" (ch. 8). Here come together the association of rapid motion with the sexual attraction between Alec and Tess, and the use of Tess's progress along the roads of Wessex as an emblem of her journey through life. Those roads are inscribed in ancient lines on the once virgin countryside as an inscription is traced out on a blank page. Both Tess's journeys and the roads themselves are versions of a cutting which is also the establishment of a new continuity, as a stick must be split to be grafted or linked on to a new shoot. The "kiss of mastery" which anticipates Alex's sexual possession of Tess is "imprint[ed]" (ch. 8), as though it were a design stamped with a die, and Tess tries to undo the kiss by "wip[ing] the spot on her cheek that had been touched by his lips" (ch. 8), as though the kiss had left a mark on her cheek. The word "graft" comes from a word meaning carving, cutting, or inscribing. "Graph" has the same etymology. With "graft" may be associated another word meaning a traced or carved-out sign, "hieroglyph." This word is used in the novel to describe Tess's naïve expectation that she will see in Alec d'Urberville "an aged and dignified face, the sublimation of all the d'Urberville lineaments, furrowed with incarnate memories representing in hieroglyphic the centuries of her family's and England's history" (ch. 5).

One more version of this motif has already been cited in chapter 1 in the passages about Alec as the "blood-red ray in the spectrum of [Tess's] young life," and about the sun's rays as "like red-hot pokers." The sun is in this novel, as in tradition generally, the fecundating male source, a principle of life, but also a dangerous energy able to pierce and destroy, as Tess, at the end of the novel, lying on the stone of sacrifice at Stonehenge, after her brief period of happiness with Angel, is wakened, just before her capture, by the first rays of the morning sun which penetrate under her eyelids: "Soon the light was strong, and a ray shone upon her unconscious form,

peering under her eyelids and waking her" (ch. 58). This association of
death and sexuality with a masculine sun had been prepared earlier in the
novel not only by the description of Alec as the blood-red ray but also,
most explicitly, by the full context of the passage describing the sun's rays:

> The sun, on account of the mist, had a curious sentient, personal
> look, demanding the masculine pronoun for its adequate ex-
> pression. His present aspect, coupled with the lack of all human
> forms in the scene, explained the old time heliolatries in a
> moment. One could feel that a saner religion had never pre-
> vailed under the sky. The luminary was a golden-haired, beam-
> ing, mild-eyed, God-like creature, gazing down in the vigour
> and intentness of youth upon an earth that was brimming with
> interest for him.
>
> His light, a little later, broke through chinks of cottage shut-
> ters, throwing stripes like red-hot pokers upon cupboards,
> chests of drawers, and other furniture within; and awakening
> harvesters who were not already astir.
>
> (ch. 14)

These passages indicate what meaning the reader should ascribe to all
the chain of red things in the novel: the red ribbon in Tess's hair; her mouth
("[Angel] saw the red interior of her mouth as if it had been a snake's"; ch.
27); those red lips with which she says the characteristic "ur" sound of her
dialect; the strawberry that Alec forces her to eat; the roses that Alec gives
her, with which she pricks her chin; the red scratches on her wrist in the
reaping scene ("as the day wears on its feminine smoothness becomes
scarified by the stubble, and bleeds"; ch. 14); the red stains made on her
arms when, in an extraordinary scene, she approaches closer and closer
under Angel's window, fascinated by his harp playing, making her way
through "tall blooming weeds emitting offensive smells" ("She went
stealthily as a cat through this profusion of growth, gathering cuckoo-
spittle on her skirts, cracking snails that were underfoot, staining her hands
with thistle-milk and slug-slime, and rubbing off on her naked arms sticky
blights which, though snow-white on the apple-tree trunks, made madder
[bright red] stains on her skin"; ch. 19; BL MS., f. 136, reads "blood-
red" instead of "madder"); the red painted signs that have already been
cited [elsewhere] ("THY, DAMNATION, SLUMBERETH, NOT"); the "unwavering
blood-colored light" reflected from the fire on the underside of the man-
telshelf (BL MS., f. 28), or the "red-coaled glow" on Tess's face (ch. 34), as
she makes her confession to Angel after their marriage; the "piece of

blood-stained paper, caught up from some meat-buyer's dust heap" which "beat[s] up and down the road," "too flimsy to rest, too heavy to fly away" (ch. 44), when Tess makes her abortive attempt to appeal to Angel's parents after he has abandoned her; the "scarlet oozing" from Alec's face after Tess has struck him with her threshing glove, "heavy and thick as a warrior's" (an ironic reminiscence of the gloves of her "armed progenitors"; ch. 47); the growing blot of blood on the ceiling, like "a gigantic ace of hearts" (ch. 56), when Alec has been murdered. All these red things are marks made by that creative and destructive energy underlying events to which Hardy gave the name "Immanent Will." This is incarnated in one form in the sun. It is also diffused in all those agents which fecundate, injure, or make signs in the triple chain of recurrent acts—copulation, physical violence, and writing—which organizes this novel. It is in accord with the deep logic of these recurrent configurations that the passage about the masculine sun is followed by a description of the reaping machine whose "two broad arms of painted wood" are "of all ruddy things that morning the brightest," as "the paint with which they were smeared, intensified in hue by the sunlight, imparted to them a look of having been dipped in liquid fire" (ch. 14). Another passage concentrates all these elements in a single sentence: "The sun was so low on that short last afternoon of the year that it shone in through a small opening and formed a golden staff which stretched across to [Tess's] skirt where it made a spot like a paint-mark set upon her" (ch. 34; BL MS., f. 271, has "permanent mark").

The novel itself is defined in the prefaces as a mark imprinted on Hardy's mind, as a die strikes a coin, and repeated or re-inscribed in the words of the text. The novel is, Hardy tells his readers in his preface to the fifth edition, "an impression, not an argument"; he has "writ[ten] down how the things of the world strike him." In his preface of 1912 he describes the subtitle as "the estimate left in a candid mind of the heroine's charac-ter," a re-enactment of the tracing of a coarse pattern on Tess's virgin flesh. Here "candid" matches "practically blank as snow," and "estimate" matches the "measure" dealt by Tess's ancestors to long-dead peasant girls and measured out again less ruthlessly to Tess by Alec. "Estimate" and "measure" suggest "ratio," "proportion," or "logic" making a design, as a throw of the dice makes a pattern or as reproduction is the dissemination of a genetic code.

The novel proper is repeated by its title, by its subtitle, by the epi-graph, and by its sequence of four prefaces or explanatory notes. These prefaces discuss the way the novel and its subtitle are repetitions. *Tess of the D'Urbervilles*, says Hardy in the note to the first edition, is "an attempt to give artistic form to a true sequence of things." The sequence existed first. The novel repeats it in a different form. "To exclaim illogically against the gods, singular or plural," he says in the preface to the fifth edition, "is not such an original sin of mine as he [Andrew Lang, who had attacked the novel] seems to imagine." The novel is the repetition of an older sin, Shakespeare's sin in *King Lear,* or the historical Gloucester's sin before that. In the preface of 1912 Hardy says that the subtitle, "A Pure Woman/Faithfully Presented," "was appended at the last moment, after reading the final proof." It is a summary of the whole, another form of duplication.

Besides calling attention to the way the book is a repetition, the prefaces are also themselves reaffirmations of the novel. They are attempts to efface it or to apologize for it which in that apology reiterate it or admit that once it is written it cannot be erased, as, within the fiction, Tess's life, once it has happened, can never not have been. The novelist in his own way repeats the fate of his heroine. Neither can escape from the reiteration of an act performed in the past. "The pages," says Hardy of the preface of 1892, "are allowed to stand for what they are worth, as something once said; but probably they would not have been written now." In the act of saying, "I would not write them now," in effect he writes them over again. In the prefatory note of 1912, speaking of the subtitle, he says *"Melius fuerat non scribere.* But there it stands." Once more, in saying "It would have been better not to have written it," he recognizes that it is ineffaceable. The proofreader's delete sign turns into a "stet." He lets it stand not so much because he wants to as because he cannot do otherwise, just as Tess cannot by any means satisfy her wish to have her life "unbe." As Hardy says in one of his poems, "Nor God nor Demon can undo the done."

The same cluster of motifs is repeated again in the epigraph for the novel from *Two Gentlemen of Verona* cited above. There sex and writing, with a reversal of the usual polarities of male and female, are joined again in the image of Hardy's "bosom" as both a bed and a writing tablet on which are written Tess's name and her story, giving her an inscribed permanence there, as things past and forgotten, in Hardy's poems, exist permanently in his memory and in the words of the poems as they are written down, printed, and reprinted. It is not Tess herself who will be lovingly protected in Hardy's bosom, but her "wounded name."

In *Tess of the D'Urbervilles* each passage is a node, a point of intersection or focus, on which converge lines leading from many other passages in the novel and ultimately including them all. Though the passage I have chosen would strike any reader as especially important, it is not the origin or end of the others. To give another example, the sun is not the chief representative of the Immanent Will in the novel. The Immanent Will exists only in its representatives, and each representative has its own irreplaceable specificity and validity. Any motif in *Tess of the D'Urbervilles* exists only in the examples of it. None of these has a sovereign explanatory function for the others. Moreover, the chains of connection or of repetition which converge on a given passage are numerous and complex. The reader can only thread his way from one element to another, interpreting each as best he can in terms of the others. It is possible to distinguish chains of connection which are material elements in the text, like the red things; or metaphors, like the figures of grafting or of writing; or covert, often etymological, associations, like the connection of grafting with writing or cutting; or thematic elements, like sexuality or murder; or conceptual elements, like the question of cause or the theory of history; or quasi-mythological elements, like the association of Tess with the harvest or the personification of the sun as a benign god. None of these chains has priority over the others as the true explanation of the meaning of the novel. Each is a permutation of the others rather than a distinct realm of discourse, as the myth of the paternal sun is a version of the dangerous power of the all-too-human Alec d'Urberville, not its explanatory archetype.

Taken together, the elements form a system of mutually defining motifs, each of which exists as its relation to the others. The reader must execute a lateral dance of interpretation to explicate any given passage, without ever reaching, in this sideways movement, a passage which is chief, original, or originating, a sovereign principle of explanation. The meaning, rather, is suspended within the interaction among the elements. It is immanent rather than transcendent. This does not mean that one interpretation is as good as another but that the meaning must be formulated not as a hierarchy, with some ur-explanation at the top, truest of the true, but as an interplay among a definable and limited set of possibilities, all of which have force, but all of which may not logically have force at once. This does not exempt the reader from seeking answers to the question of why Tess is compelled to repeat herself and others and to suffer through those repetitions. The answers, rather, must lie in the sequence itself. In its proposal and rejection of a whole set of explanations by a cause outside the sequence, and in its presentation of a repetitive chain which develops its own immanent meaning, *Tess of the D'Urbervilles* is a special version of that intertwining of the two forms of repetition which I have discussed elsewhere.

Hardy's "attempt to give artistic form to a true sequence of things" in *Tess* contains recurring images of a chain, row, or sequence. The powerful emblematic effect of topography in the novel calls attention to the linear pattern, leading the reader to think of Tess's life as her journey through the series of places where she lives. The novel, moreover, is organized as a sequence of seasons. Tess in one place sees her life as "numbers of tomorrows just all in a line," each saying, "I'm coming! Beware of me! beware of me!" (ch. 19). The motif of the series is introduced in the opening description by Parson Tringham of the d'Urberville ancestors "at Kingsbere-sub-Greenhill: rows and rows of you in your vaults, with your effigies under Purbeck-marble canopies" (ch. 1). Along these various forms of rows the reader must move, making each series, and the intertwined rope of thematic and figurative threads they make together, in one way or another into a meaningful totality.

My interpretation so far has suggested that the chains of meaning which converge on the passage describing Tess's violation are made of elements congruent with one another, as all the red things seem to mean the same thing. In fact this is not the case. The passage brings to the surface in a number of ways the method of permutation which establishes the relation among the elements in a given chain in Hardy's novel. In each new appearance the components are rearranged. The new example does not match the first, though it clearly repeats it. The relation among the links in a chain of meanings in *Tess of the D'Urbervilles* is always repetition with a difference, and the difference is as important as the repetition.

The way in which Tess's violation repeats with a difference previous events is made clear by its relation to the various models of explanation which are incorporated into the fabric of the description. These interpretations are canceled almost as soon as they are put forward, partly by their incompatibility with one another. Hardy's novels are puzzling not because they contain no self-interpretative elements, but because they contain too many irreconcilable ones. Criticism of Hardy has often erred by seizing on one element in a given novel as the single explanation of the meaning of what happens, leaving aside other explanations for which just as much textual evidence can be given. The most obvious form in *Tess of the D'Urbervilles* of that heterogeneity I consider to be characteristic of literature is the presence of multiple incompatible explanations of what happens to Tess. They cannot all be true, and yet they are all there in the words of the novel.

Part of the importance of the passage I have chosen to discuss lies in the fact that it so explicitly raises the question put before the reader, as I have said, by the book as a whole: "Why does Tess suffer so?" Various aspects of Hardy's way of presenting Tess's story keep this question insistently before the reader: the emphasis on its linear sequentiality, which implies a causal relation among the elements; the incompatibility between what Tess wills and what happens, which suggests that something outside her intention must be patterning her life. Her life, against her wishes, forms a sequence of repetitions. These give the whole a design which is a repetition of earlier fictional, historical, or mythological prototypes. The emergence of an unwilled or undesired pattern raises the question of its source. What is the originating power which causes Tess's life to fall into a symmetrical design leading her step by step to her execution? "Why was it," as the novel poses the question, " . . . there should have been traced such a coarse pattern?"

The passage describing Tess's deflowering proposes and rejects five possible answers to this question. The reason for the rejection in each case lies in the fact that though the explanatory model is duplicated by what happens to Tess, it is duplicated in the form of an ironic reversal. This invalidates the model as a straightforward explanatory cause.

The first of these anterior models is suggested by the location of Tess's violation among "the primeval yews and oaks of The Chase" (ch. 11). The Chase has been described earlier as one of the few prehistoric forests left in England. This forest, in the association of its name with hunting and in the antiquity of its trees, recalls the ancient forest that figures earlier in the novel and of which it may be said to be the displacement, the Vale of Blackmoor. Tess's home village of Marlott is located in Blackmoor. The Vale of Blackmoor was "known in former times," says the narrator. "as the Forest of White Hart, from a curious legend of King Henry III's reign, in which the killing by a certain Thomas de la Lynd of a beautiful white hart which the king had run down and spared, was made the occasion of a heavy fine" (ch. 2). Tess's violation in the Chase echoes the death of her legendary precursor, the white hart, but for Tess there is no king to spare her and to take vengeance on her violator. Rather she is victimized by men in manifold ways until her death. She takes vengeance into her own hands when she murders Alec, and thereby seals her doom and repeats that other legend, "the family tradition of the coach and murder" (ch. 57). There is an "obscure strain in the d'Urberville blood," Angel thinks as he looks down at Tess weeping with happiness on his shoulder, which predisposes them to sudden acts of violence.

Tess's re-enactment of the family tradition reverses its elements, if we take the first of Alec's versions of it, the one in which the man is a murderer. "One of the family," he tells Tess, "is said to have abducted some beautiful woman, who tried to escape from the coach in which he was carrying her off, and in the struggle he killed her—or she killed him—I forget which. Such is one version of the tale" (ch. 51). Tess's story is another version of the tale. As in its relation to the legend of the white hart, so in its relation to the family legend, the elements in the precursor event are rearranged in a new pattern with a new significance. In Henry III's time justice was done. Society was an organic fabric in which retribution could occur. In Tess's experience no secure moral or social order exists. Every reader of the novel remembers the irony of the narrator's final judgement: "'Justice' was done, and the President of the Immortals, in Aeschylean phrase, had ended his sport with Tess" (ch. 59). Not so well known is the note in Hardy's autobiography in which he says that the phrase "President of the Immortals" has no proper theological reference. It is a figurative personification of the impersonal forces that rule the universe. These forces Hardy called the Immanent Will. In that famous Aeschylean phrase, says Hardy, quoting Campbell's *Philosophy of Rhetoric*, "The forces opposed to the heroine were allegorized as a personality . . . by the use of a well-known trope, . . . 'one in which life, perception, activity, design, passion, or any property of sentient beings, is attributed to things inanimate.'"

The second interpretative model is implicitly rejected in the same way. Once again Tess's life repeats an anterior pattern, but repeats it with such a difference as to make the pattern of no use as an explanatory principle. The question in this case is the analogy between Tess's experience and the general fecundity of nature. Tess's "gentle regular breathing," as she lies asleep before Alec returns, is echoed by the "gentle roosting birds in their last nap." Her power of reproduction echoes that of "the hopping rabbits and hares" in the forest around. Part of the pathos of Tess's suffering arises from the fact that her bearing of Alec's child follows from "doing what comes naturally." Her act joins her to the general life of nature. In the magnificent reaping scene she becomes almost a part of inanimate nature as she moves rhythmically down the rows of harvested grain, "holding the corn in an embrace like that of a lover" (ch. 14), and pausing to suckle her child: "a field-woman is a portion of the field; she has somehow lost her own margin, imbibed the essence of her surrounding, and assimilated herself with it" (ch. 14).

Tess is as much a victim of man's inhumanity to natural creatures as those pheasants dying in the wood, wounded by hunters, whose necks she mercifully wrings in an episode much later in the novel (ch. 41). She is wrong to see in nature a personified reproach to her impurity:

Walking among the sleeping birds in the hedges, watching the skipping rabbits on a moonlit warren, or standing under a

> pheasant-laden bough, she looked upon herself as figure of
> Guilt intruding into the haunts of Innocence. But all the while
> she was making a distinction where there was no difference.
> Feeling herself in antagonism she was quite in accord. She had
> been made to break an accepted social law, but no law known to
> the environment in which she fancied herself such an anomaly.
> (ch. 13)

One meaning of the subtitle, "a pure woman," is a claim that Tess's
behavior has been in accord with nature. Tess, however, unlike the rabbits
and pheasants, dwells within human culture as well as within nature.
Natural behavior by human being is always more than purely natural.
Tess has broken no natural law and has done nothing different from what
the rabbits and the pheasants do, but she has been made to break an accepted social law. In this her repetition of natural behavior is a repetition
with a difference. Part of the poignancy of Tess's story lies in its demonstration of man's distance from nature. The relation of her life to its models
in nonhuman nature can neither explain nor justify what happens to her.

The third interpretative model proposed in the passage is rejected
even more decisively and with an even more bitterly ironic chiasmus:
"But, might some say, where was Tess's guardian angel? where was the
providence of her simple faith? Perhaps, like that other god of whom the
ironical Tishbite spoke, he was talking, or he was pursuing, or he was in a
journey, or he was sleeping and not to be awaked" (ch. 11). This rejects any
interpretation of what happens to Tess by way of orthodox theology, while
laying the ground for the irony in Angel Clare's name. By way of the
Biblical echo it presents Tess's situation once more as a repetition with a
difference in which the anterior model provides no satisfactory explanation of what happens to her. Just as Angel's name might lead the reader to
hope he might serve as a human embodiment of Tess's missing guardian
angel, while in fact he offers her no protection, so Tess's world as a whole is
bereft of any providential presence. Things happen to her as they happen.
They are guided from behind the scenes by no divine designer.

Tess in her simple faith is ironically not in the position of a Bible-
reading Christian nor in that of the Old Testament believer in Jehovah. She
is, rather, like the prophets of Baal, whose impotent God could not answer
their prayer for magic fire under the sacrificial bullock. Those prophets
were savagely mocked by Elijah, "the ironical Tishbite":

> And they took the bullock which was given them, and they
> dressed it, and called upon the name of Baal from morning even

until noon, saying, O Baal, hear us. But there was no voice, nor any that answered. And they leaped upon the altar which was made. And it came to pass at noon, that Elijah mocked them, and said, Cry aloud: for he is a god; either he is talking, or he is pursuing, or he is in a journey, or peradventure he sleepeth, and must be awaked. And they cried aloud, and cut themselves after their manner with knives and lancets, till the blood gushed out upon them.

(1 Kings 18:26-28)

In the Old Testament story Elijah's prayers are answered with a fire which consumes the sacrifice. In Tess's world Christianity has replaced the worship of Baal as a belief in a God absent or dead. A modern-day Elijah would be as powerless as those impotent priests of Baal. In a context repeating in a new way the elements of fire, sacrifice, and an act of violence in which blood flows, Tess's violation repeats its Biblical prototype. It repeats it with a reversal of all the Old Testament valences, offering the reader no hope of a Biblical interpretation of Tess's experience.

The ironic relation between what happens to Tess and any Biblical interpretation of it is reinforced by a second reference to a Biblical explanation of the recurrences in human experience. The divine lust for vengeance visits the sins of the fathers on the children even to the third generation. Two wrongs, for Hardy, do not make a right. There may be the "possibility of a retribution lurking in the present catastrophe." Tess may be suffering for the sins committed by her mailed ancestors. Their violence is balanced by her suffering. This evening of the score is scornfully rejected as "a morality good enough for divinities." It is good enough for beings who are by nature unjust, meting out the savage morality of an eye for an eye, a tooth for a tooth. Such a morality of retribution is "scorned by average human nature" because it "does not mend the matter." Rather than removing the coarse pattern, repairing the tear, it repeats and prolongs the rent in the fabric. The impure cannot be returned to its purity. It cannot be made once more a tissue blank as snow.

In this case too, the new exemplar repeats its model with an ironic reversal of its elements. The "measure" dealt by Alec to Tess is incommensurate with the measure dealt by Tess's ancestors to the peasant girls of their time. Tess is a true d'Urberville. Her aristocratic ancestors dealt a ruthless measure to peasant girls, as one deals a hand of cards, takes measures, or promulgates a measure in the sense of a law. The word "measure" indicates ratio or proportion. It suggests a pattern which might be numbered, accounted for mathematically, like a genetic code. The measure is here a euphemism for sexual generation. A measure is a pattern, even if only a coarse pattern. In the present repetition, however, Tess is the peasant girl who is having the same "measure" dealt to her by an imitation d'Urberville. Alec is the upstart scion of an ignoble family. He needs to graft his blood on the old, authentic line, and his act is no more than a base parody of the brutal noblesse of Tess's aristocratic ancestors. The false needs the true, but the true, it seems, also needs the false. The present event makes the ancient model into a "pattern" by duplicating it in a debased and reversed form.

The fourth interpretative model, that of "analytical philosophy," seems to be unequivocally rejected: "Why so often the coarse appropriates the finer thus, the wrong man the woman, and wrong woman the man, many thousand years of analytical philosophy have failed to explain to our sense of order" (ch. 11). "Analytical philosophy" presupposes some underlying order in the world, and some governing power determining a fitness of things. The mismatching of man and woman through the centuries can be justified according to no philosophical system. It challenges our assumption that the universe makes sense.

A more specific reference underlies the passage, as a parallel passage earlier in the novel confirms:

> We may wonder whether at the acme and summit of the human progress these anachronisms will be corrected by a finer intuition, a closer interaction of the social machinery than that which now jolts us round and along; but such completeness is not to be prophesied, or even conceived possible. Enough that in the present case, as in millions, it was not the two halves of a perfect whole that confronted each other at the perfect moment; a missing counterpart wandered independently about the earth waiting in crass obtuseness till the late time came. Out of which maladroit delay sprang anxieties, disappointments, shocks, catastrophes, and passing-strange destinies.
>
> (ch. 5)

Hardy has in mind the great comic myth, proposed by Aristophanes in Plato's *Symposium*. There was once a race of hermaphrodites , says Aristophanes, each formed of a man and a woman joined together to make a spherical and androgynous whole. This whole the gods divided. Each of the resulting hemispheres has since then wandered the world seeking to rejoin his or her counterpart. Hardy's version of the human predicament repeats this situation with a characteristic difference, a crisscrossing of the pattern like those already encountered. This crisscrossing is figured also, it happens, in the geographical movements of the heroine. The story traces Tess's series of progressions through life across the landscape of Wessex. She goes from Marlott north to Trantridge, back to Marlott, down to Talbothays in the Valley of the Great Dairies, up to Flintcomb-Ash, south again home when her father dies, further south to Sandbourne where she kills Alec, then north again to Stonehenge and Wintoncester, where she dies. Her trajectory makes a design. This design is traced out by her failure to attain union with her missing other half. For Hardy, as opposed to Plato, there is no original unity. Though there may somewhere be a matching self of the opposite sex for each person, the two can never come together at the right time and place. Life for Hardy is a wandering detour across a gap opened up in time and place by the distance between each person and his or her missing half.

Near the end of *Beyond the Pleasure Principle* Sigmund Freud also alludes to the myth from the *Symposium*. Both Hardy and Freud, with help from Plato, speculate, one in a scientific treatise, the other in a novel, that each man or woman moves forward through life repeating an unsuccessful attempt to reach again a seemingly lost primal unity. That unity may exist, however, in the counterpossibility both writers propose, only as a shadow generated by each person's imaginary original separation from his counterpart. Erotic desire is a mask for the death wish. Life is a detour on the journey toward death. For Hardy, as for Freud, only in death—not in any happy conjunction with my other half—can I escape my unappeasable desire for something which is missing.

"Thus the thing began," says the narrator of Tess's first meeting with Alec. "Had she perceived this meeting's import she might have asked why she was doomed to be seen and coveted that day by the wrong man, and not by some other man, the right and desired one in all respects—as nearly as humanity can supply the right and desired; yet to him who amongst her acquaintance might have approximated to this kind, she was but a transient impression, half forgotten" (ch. 5). For Plato, my other half was mine by right originally. For Hardy, my counterpart is met, if at all, only through a chance conjunction of two persons making their separate paths through the world. Angel Clare is Tess's most nearly proper mate. He encounters Tess by accident in the opening scene of the novel, at the May-Day dance, but the encounter fails to make a permanent impression on his memory. "Impression," the reader will remember, is a key word in the prefaces to *Tess*. If a work of literature records the transient impressions things make on the "candid" mind of the author, Tess has made but a transient impression on Angel, the man best fitted for her. The conjunction has occurred, but it has not made a deep enough impression to enter into his conscious memory, though the narrator's recording of this failure gives it the permanence of the words printed on the page. In fact, Angel's singling out of Tess from the other milkmaids, much later in the novel, in the Talbothays section, is caused, the narrator says, by his unconscious recognition that he has seen her before:

> And then he seemed to discern in her something that was familiar, something which carried him back into a joyous and unforeseeing [BL MS., f. 132: thoughtless] past, before the necessity of taking thought had made the heavens gray. He concluded that he had beheld her before; where, he could not tell. A casual encounter during some country ramble it certainly had been, and he was not greatly curious about it. But the circumstance was sufficient to lead him to select Tess in preference to the other pretty milkmaids when he wished to contemplate contiguous [BL MS., f. 132: weak] womankind.
>
> (ch. 18)

Angel's noticing of Tess at the dairy farm is experienced as a species of déjà vu. The first encounter was not even noticed, but the second makes the first into an origin. That original, since it cannot be remembered as such, even seems to belong to some fabulous or mythical past, as though it were a reminiscence from another more joyous world.

This curious mechanism of "memory" whereby the second creates the meaning of the first and makes it a first is parallel, as I have said, to Freud's interpretation of hysterical trauma. For Freud, the first episode is sexual but not understood as such at the time. The second event is innocuous, but is experienced as a repetition of the first, liberating its traumatic effect. The trauma is neither in the first nor in the second, but in the relation between them. In a similar way, Tess makes an "impression" on Angel only when he encounters her at Talbothays, but that impression is dependent for its effect on his first encounter with her, when she did not make an impression on him. In a way parallel to this, the impression made by *Tess of the D'Urbervilles* on the minds of its readers, it may be, is dependent on the chains of repetition which structure it as a text, even (or perhaps better) when the reader is not fully conscious of those chains.

If Angel's first noticing of Tess is not the first, but already a repetition, Tess's first meeting with Alec is heavy with future consequences, in spite of the fact that it is the conjunction of the coarse with the finer, the wrong man with the right woman. As the narrator affirms, "In the ill-judged execution of the well-judged plan of things the call seldom produces the comer, the man to love rarely coincides with the hour for loving. Nature does not often say 'See!' to her poor creature at a time when seeing can lead to happy doing; or reply 'Here!' to a body's cry of 'Where?' till the hide-and-seek has become an irksome, outworn game" (ch. 5). Time in this novel is this failure of fit. The narrative is generated by the division between Tess and her proper mate. This spacing opens up the field of desire through which Tess wanders, driven by her longing for her missing counterpart. This "anachronism," this bad timing, makes possible inharmonious conjunctions like that of Tess and Alec. These are displaced or deformed parodies of the true conjunction that would satisfy desire. These false encounters are the shocks and catastrophes making up Tess's destiny—the death of Prince, her violation, the murder of Alec, her union, too late, with Angel.

The novel's earlier title, "Too Late Beloved" or "Too Late, Beloved," names the maladroit delays which put off Angel's love for Tess until it is too late for it to lead to a happy union except for a brief time just before death. The proper encounter comes only when Tess is at the edge of that death for which she consciously longs. "I wish I had never been born," she tells Alec when they separate after their brief liaison (ch. 12). During her visit to the tombs of the d'Urbervilles in their long rows, Tess asks vehemently, "Why am I on the wrong side of this door!" (ch. 52). In the poem "Tess's Lament," spoken apparently at a time after Angel has deserted Tess but before she has murdered Alec, she asks once more for death, this time in the form of a complete blotting out of all memory by others that she ever existed.

Completeness is not to be prophesied, or even conceived possible, because life is incompleteness. Completeness is death. If the time and the place were right, Tess might join her counterpart. Her individual existence would then disappear. When she meets her other half, it is already "the late time." They meet across the obstacle of her loss of virginity and of her brief liaison with Alec. She is already marked with the inexpungible stigma of "impurity." That impurity expresses the generative source, the Immanent Will. It is the mark of the sun upon her. This stigma keeps Tess from reaching the unity she desires. It has an irresistible power of genetic replication. Tess can die, her child, Sorrow, can die, but the pattern her life makes tends to repeat itself in apparently compulsive recurrences that constitute her "Fate." This pattern is at once the proleptic mark of the deferred joy and at the same time evidence that the joy has not yet been reached.

A happy, innocent union, such as that between Tess and Angel after she has murdered Alec, can for Hardy, in this novel at least, take place only in the shadow of death. The unmentioned existence of the corpse of Alec stands between Tess and Angel at their moment of greatest happiness. When she and Angel are alone together during their brief idyll, she is "thrown into a vague intoxicating atmosphere at the consciousness of being together at last, with no living soul between them; ignoring that there was a corpse" (ch. 57). She accepts death as the price she must pay for that happiness. "It is as it should be," she murmurs when she is captured at Stonehenge. "Angel, I am almost glad—yes, glad! This happiness could not have lasted. It was too much. I have had enough; and now I shall not live for you to despise me!" (ch. 58). Though the "compulsion to repeat" may be, as Freud argued, a disguise of the desire for death, this desire, it seems, cannot be satisfied. It cannot be satisfied because its goal does not exist, at least not as the point of undifferentiated origin to which all living organisms seem to have a desire to return. It exists rather as a phantasm generated by the incompleteness which is the true "beginning."

The notion of fate introduces the last model according to which Tess's violation may be understood as repetition. This model at first seems to invite the reader to interpret Tess's experience according to a conventional concept of destiny. This may be the idea, expressed by Tess in "Tess's Lament," that a person's life is inscribed already in some book of fate, and only copied from a predetermined pattern in its actual living through. It may be the idea that there is a designing mind controlling Tess's actions and forcing her to follow a certain pattern in her life. Tess's virgin flesh is "doomed to receive" the traces of a "coarse pattern." The pity of her life lies in the fact that "it was to be," according to the reading of it by her neighbors.

By the time the reader has followed out the implications of the reversal of the other models, he understands that Hardy's concept of fate cannot be dissociated from the notion of chance. Each crucial event in Tess's life is like a throw of the dice that creates one of the decisive configurations of her life—the chance encounter of Tess and Angel at the beginning, or the unlucky accident of the killing of Prince which leads Tess to seek her family's fortune at Trantridge, or the meeting of Tess's father with Parson Tringham which "originates" the whole sad sequence, or the misfortune that makes Tess's confessional letter slide under the rug in Angel's room rather than reach its intended destination. Each of these events is at once fated and accidental, like the mating of genes which creates a given individual. It happens by chance, as a fortuitous conjunction, but as the sequence of such chances lengthens out to form a chain it can in retrospect be seen to make a pattern of neatly repetitive events constituting Tess's destiny.

The episodes of *Tess of the D'Urbervilles* take place in a line, each following the last. Ultimately they form a row traced out in time, just as Tess's course is traced across the roads of southern England. Each episode in Tess's life, as it occurs, adds itself to previous ones, and, as they accumulate, behold!, they make a pattern. They make a design traced through time and on the landscape of England, like the prehistoric horses carved out on the chalk downs. Suddenly, to the retrospective eye of the narrator, of the reader, and ultimately even of the protagonist herself, the pattern is there. Each event, as it happens, is alienated from itself and swept up into the design. It ceases to be enclosed in itself and through its resonances with other events becomes a sign referring to previous and to later episodes which are signs in their turn. When an event becomes a sign it ceases to be present. It becomes other than itself, a reference to something else. For this reason Tess's violation and the murder must not be described directly. They do not happen as present events because they occur as repetitions of a pattern of violence which exists only in its recurrences and has always already occurred, however far back one goes.

In one way or another most analyses of prose fiction, including most interpretations of *Tess of the D'Urbervilles*, are based on the presupposition that a novel is a centered structure which may be interpreted if that center can be identified. This center will be outside the play of elements in the work and will explain and organize them into a fixed pattern of meaning deriving from this center. Hardy's insistent asking of the question "Why does Tess suffer so?" has led critics to assume that their main task is to find the explanatory cause. The reader tends to assume that Hardy's world is in one way or another deterministic. Readers have, moreover, tended to assume that this cause will be single. It will be some one force, original and originating. The various causes proposed have been social, psychological, genetic, material, mythical, metaphysical, or coincidental. Each such interpretation describes the text as a process of totalization from the point of departure of some central principle that makes things happen as they happen. Tess has been described as the victim of social changes in nineteenth-century England, or of her own personality, or of her inherited nature, or of physical or biological forces, or of Alec and Angel as different embodiments of man's inhumanity to woman. She has been explained in terms of mythical prototypes, as a Victorian fertility goddess, or as the helpless embodiment of the Immanent Will, or as a victim of unhappy coincidence, sheer hazard, or happenstance, or as the puppet of Hardy's deliberate or unconscious manipulations.

The novel provides evidence to support any or all of these interpretations. *Tess of the D'Urbervilles*, like Hardy's work in general, is overdetermined. The reader is faced with an embarrassment of riches. The problem is not that there are no explanations proposed in the text, but that there are too many. A large group of incompatible causes or explanations are present in the novel. It would seem that they cannot all be correct. My following through of some threads in the intricate web of Hardy's text has converged toward the conclusion that it is wrong in principle to assume that there must be some single accounting cause. For Hardy, the design has no source. It happens. It does not come into existence in any one version of the design which serves as a model for the others. There is no "original version," only an endless sequence of them, rows and rows written down as it were "in some old book," always recorded from some previously existing exemplar.

An emblem in the novel for this generation of meaning from a repetitive sequence is that red sign Tess sees painted by the itinerant preacher: THY, DAMNATION, SLUMBERETH, NOT. Each episode of the novel, or each element in its chains of recurrent motifs, is like one of these words. Each is a configuration which draws its meaning from its spacing in relation to the others. In the strange notation of the sign-painter, this gap is designated by the comma. The comma is a mark of punctuation which signifies nothing in itself but punctuation, a pause. The comma indicates the spacing in the rhythm of articulation that makes meaning possible. Each episode of the novel is, like one of the words in the sign, separated from the others, but when all are there in a row the meaning emerges. This meaning is not outside the words but within them. Such is the coercive power of pre-established syntactic sequences, that a reader is able to complete an incomplete pattern of words. Tess completes in terror and shame the second sign the painter writes: THOU, SHALT, NOT, COMMIT————, and the reader knows that the relation of 'Liza-Lu and Angel will repeat in some new way the universal pattern of suffering, betrayal, and unfulfilled desire which has been established through its previous versions in the book.

Tess wanders through her life like a sleepwalker, unaware of the meaning of what she is doing. She seeks a present satisfaction which always eludes her until her final happiness in the shadow of death. Her damnation, however, slumbereth not. This "damnation" lies in the fact that whatever she does becomes a sign, takes on a meaning alienated from her intention. Hardy affirms his sense of the meaning of Tess's story not by explaining its causes but by objectively tracing out her itinerary so that its pattern ultimately emerges for the reader to see.

Hardy's notion of fatality is the reflex of his notion of chance. Out of the "flux and reflux—the rhythm of change" which "alternate[s] and persist[s] in everything under the sky" (ch. 50) emerges as if by miracle the pattern of repetitions in difference forming the design of Tess's life. Such repetitions produce similarity out of difference and are controlled by no center, origin, or end outside the chain of recurrent elements. For *Tess of the D'Urbervilles* this alternative to the traditional metaphysical concept of repetition emerges as the way the text produces and affirms its meaning. If the heterogeneity of *Wuthering Heights* lies in the way it invites the reader to seek some transcendent origin which will explain the repetitive elements the text presents, while at the same time frustrating that search, and if *Henry Esmond* shows how pervasive irony makes it impossible to decide certainly the meaning of a repetitive series, *Tess of the D'Urbervilles*, like Hardy's other novels, brilliantly explores the implications for an understanding of human life of a form of repetition which is immanent. Such a sequence is without a source outside the series. Different as are the four novels I have read so far in this book, all four are versions of the invitation, generated by the words of the novel, to believe that there is some single explanatory principle or cause, outside the sequence of repetitive elements in the text, accompanied in one way or another by a frustration of the search that belief motivates.

On the basis of this definition of immanent repetition, it is possible to identify what Hardy means by the first half of his definition of *Tess of the D'Urbervilles* as "an attempt to give artistic form to a true sequence of things." The artistic form is the novelist's interpretation of the events. This interpretation does not falsify the events, but it imposes meaning on them by reading them in a certain way, as a sentence may have entirely different meanings depending on how it is articulated. The meaning is there and not there. It is a matter of position, of emphasis, of spacing, of punctuation. In the preface of 1892 Hardy recognizes the revolutionary effect such a new emphasis may have. It reverses the usual positions of value. To be led by a new "sentiment" of human worth or meaning to call the "impure" the "pure" may lead to an overturning of the usual relations of possession and dominance in society. The chain of family and social connections may be upset by something that begins in a passing impression. The adverse critics of Tess, said Hardy in this preface, that to the fifth edition,

> may have causes to advance, privileges to guard, traditions to keep going; some of which a mere tale-teller, who writes down how the things of the world strike him, without any ulterior intentions whatever, has overlooked, and may by pure inadver-

tence have run foul of when in the least aggressive mood. Perhaps some passing perception, the outcome of a dream hour,
would, if generally acted on, cause such an assailant consider-
able inconvenience with respect to position, interests, family,
servant, ox, ass, neighbour, or neighbour's wife . . . So densely is
the world thronged that any shifting of positions, even the best
warranted advance, galls somebody's kibe. Such shiftings often
begin in sentiment, and such sentiment sometimes begins in
a novel.

In his quietly ironic way, Hardy is claiming a powerfully subversive
effect for his novel. When by "pure inadvertence" he wrote the novel and
summarized its impression on his candid mind by giving it the subtitle "A
Pure Woman/Faithfully Presented," he initiated a shifting of positions, like
the altered emphasis on words in a sentence. This shifting would, if acted
on, ultimately rearrange the chain of power relationships in society.

Attention is insistently called to the act of reading, in the broad sense
of deciphering, throughout *Tess*. One way is the many examples of false
interpretation which are exposed by the narrator. These include the comic
example of the bull who thought it was Christmas Eve because he heard
the Nativity Hymn, or the more serious dramatization of Angel's infatua-
tion with Tess and his interpretation of her as like Artemis or like Demeter
(ch. 20), or the description of Tess's "idolatry" of Angel (ch. 34), or Tess's
false reading of nature as reproaching her for her impurity. All interpretation is the imposition of a pattern by a certain way of making cross-
connections between one sign and those which come before and after. Any
interpretation is an artistic form given to the true sequence of things.
Meaning in such a process emerges from a reciprocal act in which both the
interpreter and what is interpreted contribute to the making or the finding
of a pattern. The notion that interpretation is both invention and discovery
is neatly expressed in a passage in *The Life of Thomas Hardy*: "As, in looking
at a carpet, by following one colour a certain pattern is suggested, by following another colour, another; so in life the seer should watch that pattern
among general things which his idiosyncrasy moves him to observe, and
describe that alone. This is, quite accurately, a going to Nature; yet the
result is no mere photograph, but purely the product of the writer's own
mind." To add a new interpretation to the interpretation already proposed
by the author is to attach another link to the chain of interpretations. The
reader takes an impression in his turn. He represents to himself what already exists purely as a representation. To one purity the reader adds a

subsequent purity of his own. This is Hardy's version of the notion of multiple valid but incompatible interpretations I am proposing in this book. I would myself put greater stress, however, as Hardy himself does in the passage in *Tess* with which I shall end this chapter, on the coercive power of the sequence itself to determine the interpretation, though it may be a complex and disonant reading which is imposed, a reading combining incompatibilites which all demand to be recognized as valid by the reader.

In *Tess of the D'Urbervilles*, in any case, the narrator always presents not only the event with its "objective" elements, but also his interpretation of the event. At the same time he shows his awareness that the interpretation is "purely" imposed not inherent, except as it is one possibility among a limited repertoire of others. An example would be the "objective" description of the sun casting its beams on Tess. This is first interpreted as like the act of a god, but that interpretation is then ironically undercut: "His present aspect . . . explained the old time heliolatries in a moment" (ch. 14). The narrator's act in not only describing the true sequence of things but also giving it artistic form is shown as what it is by its doubling within the text in the interpretative acts of the characters. The narrator always sees clearly what is "subjective" in Tess's reading of her life, but this insight casts back to undermine his own readings. These multiple acts of interpretation are not misinterpretations in relation to some "true" interpretation. Each telling, even the most clear-sighted one, is another reading in its turn. The bare "reality" Angel sees when he falls out of love with Tess is as much an interpretation as the transfiguration of the world he experiences when he sees her as a goddess and the world as irradiated by her presence.

The power of readings to go on multiplying means that Tess's wish to be "forgotten quite" cannot be fulfilled. The chain of interpretations will continue to add new links. Tess can die, but the traces of her life will remain, for example in the book which records the impression she has made on the narrator's imagination. Her life has a power of duplicating itself which cancels the ending her failure to have progeny might have brought. The life of her sister will be, beyond the end of the book, another repetition with a difference of the pattern of Tess's life. Beyond that, the reader comes to see, there will be another, and then another, ad infinitum. If the novel is the impression made on Hardy's candid mind by Tess's story, the candid reader is invited to receive the impression again in his turn, according to that power of a work of art to repeat itself indefinitely to which the novel calls attention in a curious passage concerning Tess's sensitivity to music. Here is a final bit of evidence that Hardy saw the principle of repetition, in life as in art, as impersonal, immanent, and self-proliferating rather than as controlled by any external power, at least once a given repeatable sequence gets recorded in some form of notation or "trace." The "simplest music" has "a power over" Tess which can "well-nigh drag her heart out of her bosom at times" (ch. 13). She reflects on the strange coercive effect church music has on her feelings: "She thought, without exactly wording the thought, how strange and godlike was a composer's power, who from the grave could lead through sequences of emotion, which he alone had felt at first, a girl like her who had never heard of his name, and never would have a clue to his personality" (ch. 13). In the same way, *Tess of the D'Urbervilles*, as long as a single copy exists, will have its strange and godlike power to lead its readers through some version of the sequences of emotion for which it provides the notation.

Pure Tess: Hardy on Knowing a Woman

Kathleen Blake

From the title page, the reader knows Hardy's heroine as Tess of the d'Urbervilles and as "A Pure Woman," in other words, as individual and as pure abstraction. The novel's title and subtitle introduce a dialectic of knowledge which is shown to generate both good and ill, Tess's charm and her tragedy. This dialectic shapes theme, imagery, and allusion, narrative structure, and dramatic interaction, and it also makes itself eloquently felt throughout in Hardy's own language about his heroine. It even permeates the language of critics responding to the novel. At stake are Hardy's ideas about knowledge of the beautiful and the beloved, and, as a novel about knowing a woman, *Tess* offers his finest exposition of these ideas.

Hardy's post-romantic historical moment as well as his own reading and temperament inducted him into the epistemological wars whose battle lines are laid out by Hume and Kant. Kant takes up arms against Hume's characterization of experience as a mere aggregate of perceptions and instead declares the power of the mind to legislate experience. Hardy's fascination with eighteenth- and nineteenth-century philosophers of understanding and their notable literary heir, Shelley, has been pointed out by Tom Paulin in his study of the writer's poetry. This epistemological interest is well represented in a picture Hardy once drew; sketching a landscape where he had danced with a girl, he superimposed a pair of giant eyeglasses to depict the contingency of reality upon the focal powers of the observer's eyes. And he says in *Tess* that "the world is only a psychological phenomenon, and what [things] seemed they were."

From *Studies in English Literature, 1500–1900* 22 (1982). © 1981 by William Marsh Rice University.

Of abiding interest to Hardy is apprehension of the general in relation to the particular within the seeming that makes reality, and the way a woman is apprehended provides a measure of this dialectic which reveals its complexity. And so in *Tess* he explores the question: what happens when the object of knowledge is also the object of aesthetic response and of love? He finds what happens full of delight and danger.

The novel's title names the particular and attaches it to the universal in the subtitle. Tess bears a proper name as a unique person, while she is universalized as a pure woman. In defending his controversial subtitle in the preface to the fifth and subsequent editions of the novel, Hardy suggests connotations of the word "pure" that critics had missed. He says, "They ignore the meaning of the word in Nature, together with all aesthetic claims upon it, not to mention the spiritual interpretation afforded by the finest side of their own Christianity." This whole statement is more provocative than clear, and I believe that the final reference to spirituality aims more at scoring a debater's point than anything else, in that it allows Hardy to capitalize by means of irony on a meaning overlooked by his Christian critics. Many such critics had balked at attributing purity to a fornicator, unwed mother, sometimes religious skeptic, a wife who rejoins her former lover, a murderess. Tess failed to impress them with ethical purity, judged according to religious doctrine, erotic morality, or the law of the land. But, dissatisfied with commonplace understanding of his phrase, Hardy hints at wider, alternate meanings. In the case of this subtitle, signification does vary profoundly as a function of inflection. "A púre woman" does not equal "a pure wóman" (while "a púre wóman" may go either way). The first proclaims Tess a woman of certain character; the second proclaims her a woman, as though placing her within a natural and aesthetic class, as though linking her appeal to a general concept of woman's place in nature's scheme. In suggesting the connotation of natural and aesthetic purity in his preface, Hardy moves the meaning toward a new realm, that of the archetypal, essential, ideal, generic.

Though Hardy hints at such factors in Tess's purity, I cannot claim that he usually uses the word "pure" with these connotations. His critics might have defended their interpretation by pointing to the author's habitual and quite ordinary presentation of purity as an erotic characteristic, as equivalent to maidenhood, the "pure and chaste." This meaning hovers behind Angel Clare's notion of the "spotless," "unsullied," that is, sexually "intact" state. Alec d'Urberville shifts the meaning somewhat. As he sees it, Tess need not be physically intact to remain psychologically "unsmirched" by erotic experience. Still, his meaning involves a notion of erotic morality. Indeed, J. T. Laird's study of the novel's development through manuscript and published versions reveals the easy interchangeability, for Hardy, of the words "chastity" and "purity." Hardy is undeniably concerned with the erotic issue in Tess's case. His revisions reveal such concern. For instance, in later versions he takes care to downplay the heroine's sensual responsiveness and culpability, while emphasizing Angel's attraction to her specifically virginal appeal. Hardy makes Tess an even purer woman, in this sense. Critics might have claimed justification for their moral, and more particularly erotic standard of assessment.

Very few have apprehended purity in any other way. Among these few, D. H. Lawrence calls Tess a self-establishing aristocrat and in that sense "pure-bred." J. Hillis Miller calls parenthetical attention to the word "pure" and allows us to see that, like Lawrence's phrase "pure-bred," certain phrases of Hardy's such as "pure inadvertence" and "purely the product of the writer's own mind" connote the entire, integral, and essential. In the novel itself the most significant sample of such a meaning appears in Hardy's description of Tess as "a field-woman pure and simple." The passage strips her of individuality to make her a figure in the landscape, and it departs from ethical/erotic signification. The phrase itself does not propose that a field-woman is pure and simple; it proposes that she is a field-woman and nothing but a field-woman. It asserts very nearly the same thing as an early characterization of Tess: "she was a fine and picturesque country girl, and no more." In such a manner may the subtitle suggest the meaning—a woman and nothing but a woman, unspotted, unsullied, unsmirched by particularity—while the title specifies the particular woman by her own name. Tess presents the paradoxical spectacle of the "*almost* standard woman"(emphasis mine). On the one hand, she is a being for whom "the universe itself only came into being . . . on the particular day in the particular year in which she was born." On the other hand, she is "a visionary essence of woman—a whole sex condensed into one typical form."

The novel's hero, Angel Clare, favors the latter, purist point of view. As we know, Hardy shaped Angel partly from his understanding of Shelley, as he did Jocelyn Pierston in *The Well-Beloved* (1897). It is worthwhile to look at Walter Bagehot's portrait of the poet since it made a strong early impression on Hardy and may well have influenced his presentation of these Shelley-like heroes, setting him to contemplate the sort of purity in women desired by such men. Admiring Shelley, Bagehot also criticizes him as an idealist and simplifier in love, as in his other passions, so that his poetry expresses desire for all women in one rather than for any one woman. In his analysis of the Shelleyan experience of love for a single, unvarying figure under many apparitions, Bagehot seems to point Hardy toward the novelistic fantasia of *The Well-Beloved*, with its Shelleyan epigraph (from *Laon and Cythna*), "One shape of many names." This novel follows its hero's infatuations with serial copies of his single idea of the feminine. Bagehot finds such a passion intense at the expense of complexity or potential for development. He perhaps seeds Hardy's mind with a definition of purity and a line of thought leading to *Tess* and its subtitle when he calls the beloved of a Shelley poem "the pure object of the essential passion." Here "pure" exempts the beloved not only from erotic but from *any* adulteration. As aesthetic and romantic object, she becomes generic for her gender.

II

"A field-man is a personality afield; a field-woman is a portion of the field; she has somehow lost her own margin, imbibed the essence of her surrounding, and assimilated herself with it." This is another way of calling her a field-woman pure and simple, and such a notion of purity enters into Hardy's fascination throughout *Tess* with loss of margin, that is, with diffusion of uniqueness in favor of generic status. Hardy examines the trade-off between gain and loss in this transaction. Thus he points out the field-woman's "charm," while the novel as a whole subjects the sources and consequences of such charm to a probing critique.

While a woman's release from personality to become a portion of the field, an "essence of woman," or "soul at large," is the most significant mode of marginlessness treated, there are a number of others contributing to the novel's theme. For example, alcohol breaks down margins and offers pleasing expansion beyond petty, everyday identity. The imbibers at Rolliver's Inn find that "their souls expanded beyond their skins, and spread their personalities warmly through the room." In the same way, the Saturday-night revelers of Trantridge reel home liberated from the confines of self into harmony with natural forces, "themselves and surrounding nature forming an organism of which all the parts harmoniously and joyously interpenetrated each other." In a lovely image, the moonlit, misty halos that waver round their unsteady heads, compounded of the light, the dewy air, and the fumes of their own breathing, spread these men and women abroad into the night. No longer Car Darch, Nancy, and their partners, they merge with the atmosphere, and nature "seemed harmoniously to mingle with the spirit of wine."

Nature, like wine, can gratify the soul by drawing it forth from its margin. Tess seeks out the hour between day and night whose balanced light lets loose the spirit and allows it to wander "an integral part of the scene." "Our souls can be made to go outside our bodies when we are alive," Tess says, and cultivates the feeling by gazing at the stars. As dawn illumination makes Tess look like a "soul at large," and as a moonlit mist allows the Tantridge revelers to join with the night, other effects of light serve to blur the psychological edges. The dancers of Trantridge dim into the nebulosity of a warm atmosphere of candle-lit sweat and peat-dust. The merge with the natural scene amidst a sort of "vegeto-human-pollen," and become nature gods, figures of Pan whirling Syrinx, Lotis attempting to elude Priapus.

Supporting the idea and imagery of marginlessness, a system of mythological allusions drawn from nature cults metamorphoses the particular into the general throughout the novel, as seen in the opening pageant of the Marlott club-walking. Here women of the village re-enact a timeless Cerealia. Their white dresses unify them into group identity and release them to some extent from the "real" into the "ideal." Much criticism has been devoted to such mythic patterning, as well as to the animal imagery that assimilates Tess to nature. In the same vein, Angel and Tess converge like two streams at Talbothay's Dairy, and the entire sequence is famous for its humano-natural convergences. The pair becomes by implication another generic "instalment" of young lovers like any other springtime "instalment of flowers, leaves, nightingales, thrushes, finches, and such ephemeral creatures."

In sex we see one of nature's strongest means of diffusing unique personality. Hence Hardy's strange narrative device of triplicating Tess in the other dairymaids who fall in love with Angel. According to "Nature's Law," "the differences which distinguished them as individuals were abstracted by this passion, and each was but portion of one organism called sex." It has distressed many readers, but Tess herself seems to be partly duplicated and replaced in Angel's heart by her surviving sister Liza Lu, in accordance with the abstracting law of love.

Nature's power of duplication, or triplication, figures elsewhere as temporal repetition. Hence the novel's preoccupation with history, especially in the form of d'Urberville family history. Like multiplication of those in love or loved, repetition of the doings of all who went before seems to erode autonomy, and Tess finds this loss of margin sad instead of welcome. Hardy makes repetition structural to his novel by introducing tales parallel to Tess's round Dairyman Crick's table, and many critics have stressed the ballad origin of her story.

Throughout the novel the marginless state takes different forms, both attractive and disturbing. In a landscape description on the final page marginlessness appears again. Here at the end Tess has symbolically lost her margin by suggested merging with the sister who takes her place at Angel's side. Just so, the landscape extends itself by means of a characteristically limit-dissolving light, and the pair gazes at "landscape beyond landscape, till the horizon was lost in the radiance of the sun hanging above it." This description of a boundless panorama oddly parallels a description of the mental viewpoint of the stranger Angel meets in Brazil, who persuades him to take the long view of Tess's moral breach: "to his cosmopolitan mind such deviations from the social norm, so immense to domesticity, were no more than are the irregularities of vale and mountain-chain to the whole terrestrial curve." And in a comparable description Tess herself reveals panoramic possibilities, a unity of infinite extension like a limitless landscape, for her eyes do not confine themselves in color to black, blue, gray, or violet, but present "rather all those shades together, and a hundred others—, . . . shade beyond shade—tint beyond tint."

Of course, I must reach a turn in my argument with these examples of marginless vistas, for no one can forget the counter-examples of vividly localized landscapes created by Hardy in *Tess*. He describes closely hilled-in and utterly distinct valleys. Blackmoor Vale is intrinsically different from the Vale of the Little Dairies. The two dairy valleys could not contrast more strikingly with the Chase and Flintcomb-Ash. Not even the train joins these separate locales, and Hardy insists that "every village has its idiosyncrasy, its constitution, often its own code of morality."

Just as Hardy closes in his boundless landscapes, so he indicates constraints on each of the previously mentioned marginless states. Without alcohol souls again contract within their skins. Nature sometimes refuses to intermingle and harmonize with the feelings and thus blur the line dividing scene and figure, as when Tess's arrival produces no impression at all on Blackmoor Vale. Only approximately mythic, the club-walking female votaries wear white gowns which a bright sun reveals to be of noticeably different shades and cuts, and in these women "ideal and real clashed slightly." Pans and Syrinxes resume ordinary personal identities as Car Darch, Nancy, and other Tantridge locals. Tess and Angel do not complete as standard an "instalment" of nature's springtime scenario as the birds and flowers do, for aberration marks their love. The generalizing power of sex does not carry the other dairymaids into actual equivalence with Tess, nor does 'Liza Lu adequately replace her, as many readers have felt. Tess only partly recapitulates stock family traits. She shares some of the fatalistic passivity of the d'Urbervilles and seems destined to repeat their violence, but she does not inherit her father's foolish vanity nor her mother's fecklessness and cheer. While Tess's history repeats traditional folklore materials, personal experience give them very personal meaning — "What was comedy to [others] was tragedy to her."

Just one page after Hardy calls Tess a field-woman who merges with the field and yields her own margin, he forcefully reconfines her within herself. With her baby and no husband, she occupies those fields as a "stranger and alien." Much of the book shows how far Tess diverges from the field-woman pure and simple.

A parallel exists between this individuation of Tess and another example of human individuation in the book, and in this parallel lies an important commentary. Hardy presents in his rustics a seemingly collective "Hodge," whose generic oneness disappears upon closer inspection. We soon realize that each "walked in his own individual way the road to dusty death." Explaining his convictions about Hodge in an article on "The Dorsetshire Labourer," Hardy observes of rustic laborers that "the artistic merit of their old condition is scarcely a reason why they should have continued in it. . . . It is too much to ask them to remain stagnant and old-fashioned for the pleasure of romantic spectators." This suggests the "artistic" appeal of generalizations about Hodge, thus illuminating Hardy's reference to the "aesthetic" dimension of purity in the preface to *Tess*. Placing such purity in a problematical light, the statement provides a critical gloss on the "charm" seen in the field-woman who loses her margin to form part of the field. The "Dorsetshire Labourer" passage judges such artistically agreeable class grouping as the wrongful imposition of the spectator's eye, distorting in a way that does disservice to its object.

Thus Tess, like Hodge, may lack a certain charm when viewed as only an individual, but when viewed as someone released from the margins of individuality into pure womanhood, she gains charm at a certain risk. That risk dominates the drama that unfolds between Tess and Angel Clare.

III

Certain statements by Hardy concerning perception serve to introduce his critique of Angel's attitude toward Tess. On the one hand, Hardy lacks misgivings about the truth-value of perception legislated by the categories of the perceiver's mind. As may be inferred from his declarations of the impressionistic nature of his on work, he surrenders without protest the possibility of reliable mental access to things-in-themselves. On the other hand, Hardy does have misgivings about the impact on the Tess or the Hodge mentally modified in the name of the artistic, aesthetic, charming, and in this way made subject to another's subjectivity. Thus a striking passage in *The Well-Beloved* describes the rolling together into one composite essence of all the bones of the drowned in Deadman's Bay and the single roar made by these surf-rolled bones in the listening ear. Yet the passage makes the roar a shriek, for those joined in death seem to call out to some good god to disunite them from their grisly idealist oneness. No more than these dead men distressed by their loss of individuality in the minds of those who thrill to the composite music of their bones does Tess always relish or gain by being appreciated as a pure woman. Hardy examines the meeting point of epistemology, aesthetics, and love. He shows that knowledge of the beloved and the beautiful is liable to be specially compromised. He shows the special danger of appreciation, for it may dissipate the desire to know more.

The problem is, Angel's infatuated taste makes him dispense with further knowledge. Appreciating Tess "ideally and fancifully," he "subdue[s] . . . the substance to the conception" and "drops the defects of the real" in favor of an ideal. Finding Tess lovely and loving her, he considers corporeal absence almost more appealing than presence. He regularly renders her a type in his mind: archetypal milkmaid, "virginal daughter of Nature," "daughter of the soil," representative of primitive consciousness untouched by modern doubt, and perfect sample for his contemplation of "contiguous womankind." It is true, he sometimes thinks he delights in her for her very self rather than, for instance, the things he has told his family she represents. One occasion shows his capacity to imagine Tess's apprehension of the world from within her own center of self, and, another time, he tries to project her viewpoint as one different from his own as that of a man. However, the crisis of their relationship reveals his habit of generalization when it comes to Tess and his commitment to her purity in the erotic sense *and* as a being so summed up by his conception of her that she must remain pure of any particular experience worth mentioning. Seeing Tess as essence and type, Angel cannot admit the relevance of experience for her, and so he refuses to hear her confession about her past affair with Alec. Once confronted by Tess's un-intactness, Angel's penchant for generalization intensifies, and he casts the fallen Tess as the typical peasant woman and representative of a decadent family, in contrast to the idealized "new-sprung child of nature" and example of "rustic innocence" he had expected. Significantly, he inveighs against "womankind in general." Angel typecasts Tess in terms of class, family, nature, and sex, but sexual typing exercises the most powerful sway. The novel stresses it by making the drama hinge on the issue of erotic purity, which is definitive for women but not for men—Angel's own un-intact state bothers him very little. His horror of Tess's un-intactness bespeaks his allegiance to the purity of the generic as such, as well as to the feminine principle of erotic purity that furnishes the dramatic test.

Tess usually resists imposition of generic classification upon her specificity. Even though she does sometimes enjoy release from self, as in contemplating nature, she is no addict of the marginless experience. (She doesn't drink, for one thing, and dislikes repeating stock traits, hereditary or folkloristic.) She resents being understood as "every woman" by Alec and responds angrily by exclaiming, "Did it never strike your mind that what every woman says some women may feel?" Just so, when Angel perceives her as a "soul at large" and calls her by the names of female deities as if she presented a "visionary essence," a "typical form" of woman, Tess wants none of it: " 'Call me Tess,' she would say askance." In successive revisions Hardy gives increasing point to this reply by making Tess speak it at first softly and simply but finally askance. She wants to be loved for herself and not for the image superimposed on her. Sadly she realizes, "she you love is not my real self, but one in my image," and this same thought gives rise to a moment of self-pity for ill use. She comes to judge Angel's condemnation as reflective of his fastidious mind more than her own fault.

For her own part, she is slow to consider people in absolute terms. Certainly, Hardy allows for some typing by Tess of Angel, of a man by a woman. She idolizes him during their courtship, though "Angel Clare was far from all that she thought him." And she exposes a set notion of masculinity when she values Angel for *not* fulfilling it. However, Hardy distinguishes between the attitudes of hero and heroine by calling Angel's love more insistently idealizing, while Tess's exhibits more "impassioned thoroughness." She even prefers not to reduce her enemy to a type. One might suppose that Alec's offenses against her, the diabolism of the scenes in which Hardy places him, and his own Satanic self-references would invite Tess to view him as the devil, but she refuses to do so: "I never said you were Satan, or thought it. I don't think of you in that way at all." Reluctant to be the pure woman, Tess is reluctant to regard even the man who drives her to murder as pure devil.

Tess is the greatest among a number of Hardy's works concerned with the loose fit between type and individual. For instance, the poem "The Milkmaid" treats the difference between the milkmaid's seeming embodiment of nature and her actual artificiality of spirit, and "The Beauty" treats the difference between the stock beauty of a woman's face and her personal sense of herself. Like Tess, the speaker in "The Pedigree" hates the thought that, while feeling "I am I," one only exemplifies hereditary traits. A similar thought dismays the dead in "Intra Sepulchrum." In life they considered themselves unique, but once in the grave they realize that, to others, they must have appeared to be quite commonly fashioned. Typing by sex draws Hardy's attention in a number of novels. Whether to explain Paula Power's timidity by her sex or by her temperament, for example, gives the hero pause in *A Laodicean* (1881). Hardy's distrust of sexual generalizations appears as early as in *Far from the Madding Crowd* (1874) in a passage on Boldwood's habit of "deeming as essentials of the whole sex the accidents of the single one of their number he had ever closely beheld." Hardy shows such distortion turning dangerous in *Tess of the D'Urbervilles*. In fact, he shows how dangerous it becomes just because it is so pleasant. Delighting to regard the particular Tess as an expression of the universal, Angel delays knowing better what pleases him so much, and the delay proves disastrous.

IV

However, the novel incurs a danger comparable to the one it exposes. That is, many critics complain about Angel in terms roughly like mine in the last section, but should we also be complaining about his creator? Hardy generalizes about Tess and women almost as incautiously as Angel does. After all, he is the one who calls Tess a field-woman pure and simple and maintains that such a woman loses her margin to form part of the landscape while a field-man remains a personality afield. And he is the one who calls such a woman charming. His imagery and allusions assimilate Tess to nature and nature myths as animal and goddess. As a case in point, Hardy and not Angel "apotheosizes" Tess as a "divine personage" in the famous baptism scene. He presents her to the view of her brothers and sisters, and the reader, by the light of a candle that "abstracted from her form and features the little blemishes which sunlight might have revealed," "transfiguring" her, rendering her regal and divine, purifying her into "a thing of immaculate beauty." Of course, he does remind us that Tess's apotheosis involves seeing by a certain light quite as much as it involves Tess-in-herself. And Hardy may be said to de-apotheosize his heroine in the treatment immediately following. When he describes Tess's burial of the infant, homely little blemishes return. Tess garnishes the grave with a bunch of flowers in a container in no wise abstracted or transfigured, a "Keelwell's Marmalade" jar. Throughout the novel Hardy alternates between idealizing and particularizing Tess. By alternating in this way while also calling attention to it, he may be said to exhibit while also examining the epistemological sources of her tragedy.

Yet in his own language Hardy can seem more intrepid than self-examining. He often generalizes about women surprisingly for a man who had pondered the fairness of it in earlier novels, who had analyzed the potential distortions in a comment on Boldwood and dramatized the real harm that could be done through the story of Angel and Tess. Without apparent self-consciousness Hardy refers in *Tess* to "the woman's instinct to hide," to "feminine loss of courage," to "feminine hope" that is obstinately recuperative, to the usual "feminine feelings of spite and rivalry." Sentences such as the following appear: "like the majority of women, she accepted the momentary presentment as if it were the inevitable"; "let the truth be told—women do as a rule live through such humiliations"; "she had gathered . . . sufficient of the incredulity of modern thought to despise flash enthusiasms; but, as a woman, she was somewhat appalled." As phrases, "like the majority of women" and "women do as a rule" clearly generalize. The last-quoted sentence does so more subtly and equivocally. Does "as a woman, she was somewhat appalled" assign her feeling to her as a representative of her sex or as a particular individual who happens to be female? Imagine an apparently parallel sentence reading, "he had gathered sufficient of the incredulity of modern thought to despise flash enthusiasms; but, as a man, he was somewhat appalled." Parallelism is only apparent here, for "man" would signify either a particular individual who happens to be male or else a representative of the human race. The word "man" and the masculine pronoun are often said to function generically. But in standing for mankind as well as for a single man, they do not implicate masculinity. Unless strongly conditioned by context, these words do not act as gender generics since their ambiguous reference vitiates their power of specifically sexual generalization. But "woman" and "she" undergo no such vitiation.

Hardy gives signs of some awareness of the shaping or constraining force of language upon apprehension. For instance, he cites with interest Comte's statement concerning the difficulty of expressing new ideas in existing language, that is, the vehicle for existing conceptualization. The conventional may be so conveniently expressed as to discourage more original response, which inspires Hardy's amusing characterization of Angel Clare's conventional brothers as men who express more than they observe. Hardy's sensitivity to the power of labels appears in his dislike of the word and concept Hodge and in his bemusement over his own creation of a concept in creating (or re-creating from ancient usage) the word Wessex. His seriousness about the need for new language to express new thoughts appears in the striking coinages and syntactical inventions of his poetry. And he indicates critical awareness of the sexual concepts built into language in this observation of Bathsheba's in *Far from the Madding Crowd*: "it is difficult for a woman to define her feelings in language which is chiefly made by men to express theirs."

Hardy does not entirely free himself from masculine language, but his generalizations about women grow less casual and copious as novel follows novel. Practically every folly of Bathsheba Everdene manages in the telling to reflect on her sex. On just one page, she "had too much womanliness to use her understanding to the best advantage," and "she loved Troy in the way that only self-reliant women love when they abandon their self-reliance." In contrast, Sergeant Troy is allowed to represent only himself by his sins. Even in *Far from the Madding Crowd* Hardy passes glancing judgment on the validity of typecasting by sex, but *Tess of the D'Urbervilles* really scrutinizes the sexual typing that plays havoc with a woman's life. In his verbal habits Hardy only partly separates himself from Angel's mental ones, while the irony of the overlap draws attention and actually extends the novel's interest as a commentary on the heroine as pure woman. It dramatizes the author's susceptibility to an outlook shown to be dangerous in the hero. I believe *Tess* must have prepared the way toward the more fully feminist *Jude the Obscure* (1896). This work still hazards generalizations about women; it speculates as to whether Sue Bridehead succumbs to womanly conventionality, or lack of courage, or irrationality. But the novel renders these generalizations so multiple and contradictory as to throw each other into question if not to cancel each other out.

V

This is not to say that Hardy condemns generalization altogether. In his literary notebook he cites Herbert Spencer on biological classification. To group particular organisms into general groups is distortive, yet such grouping is useful and necessary "so long as the distorted form is not mistaken for the actual form . . . giving to the realities a regularity which does not exist." In his essay on "The Profitable Reading of Fiction" Hardy disdains an art of merely photographic particularity and values creative transformation of the subject more than the subject itself. He shares Taine's approval of "imaginations which create and transform." In fact, according to the preface to *The Dynasts* (1903), he relishes an essence-abstracting art such as mumming and aims at parallel effect by means of "dreamy conventional gestures" and an "automatic style." In any dramatization of *The Dynasts* "gauzes or screens to blur outlines might still further shut off the actual." This hypothetical stage direction recalls various treatments of marginlessness in *Tess* and indicates Hardy's penchant for departicularization. Similarly, Florence Emily Hardy's biography records his speculations on a future fiction that would delineate visible essences and abstract thoughts, "the Realities to be the true realities of life, hitherto called abstractions. The old material realities to be placed behind the former, as shadowy accessories." These opinions reveal a devotee of the ideal like Jocelyn Pierston and Angel Clare.

As a matter of fact, Hardy believes that two of the best things life has to offer, both love and art, depend on idealization. Florence Emily Hardy cites a very interesting note of Hardy's about love: "It is the incompleteness that is loved. . . . This is what differentiates the real one from the imaginary. . . . A man sees the Diana or the Venus in his Beloved, but what he loves is the difference." This formulates a dialectic of the general and the particular in the lover's understanding. The general may be said to initiate the experience rather than derive from it, since the type must be viewed in the woman for her departure from type as an individual to be known and loved. Hardy brings this formulation to life in his novel through the attraction of his hero, himself, and, by invitation, his reader toward Tess as the "almost standard woman." As the almost pure woman she commands love.

Such cognitive dynamics in love make it unstable and even treacherous, and Angel Clare's example might seem to recommend letting the standard go and relieving Tess of the painful consequences of only almost fulfilling it. But *The Well-Beloved* shows that not only is love lost but aesthetic response, too, in the loss of a standard. Its Shelleyan hero is finally cured of his mainly disastrous erotic idealism. The single, absolute image of the well-beloved meets extinction in the course of Pierston's symbolic illness, and afterwards he finds himself able to respond to a woman in her manifold particularity, frailties and all. He enters into her situation and viewpoint and takes an interest in her for herself as he has never done before. However, loss attends this gain, for he finds "I can no longer love." Besides that, he finds himself losing artistic inspiration as a sculptor. According to Hardy, then, response to loveliness as well as love as love itself depends on idealization, which may, in turn, prove over-dominant and destructive. This helps to clarify his prefatory comment on Tess as pure woman, aesthetically understood.

VI

Whereas Hardy points out the charm as well as the clash that may be seen in the interplay of ideal and real, critics of the novel tend to focus on ideal *or* real. Actually, most express a preference for a real Tess and judge Hardy according to his failure or success in embodying her, while a number of them simultaneously betray their own attraction toward an ideal Tess in their language about her. Suspicious of Hardy's sexual generalizations, Ellen Moers condemns him for basing his novel on a cultural stereotype, an "all-purpose heroine," a "fantasy of almost pornographic dimensions." John Bayley takes a milder tone but also observes that a "male fantasy" plays a part in the creation of Tess. He credits Hardy with only involuntary insights into his heroine's subjectivity. Taking the other side, Arnold Kettle and Dorothy Van Ghent praise Hardy for particularizing Tess. According to Kettle, he displays "mistrust of . . . all ways of thinking that give abstract ideals or principles . . . priority over the actual needs of specific human situations," and, according to Van Ghent, he shows artistic commitment to "the concrete body of experience," "body of particularized life," and "concrete circumstances of experience, real as touch." Van Ghent contrasts interestingly to Bayley, for while he finds stereotype-shattering insights into Tess's uniqueness occasional and unintended, she considers abstracting, philosophical passages to be the intrusions. The two agree, though, and exemplify much critical response in their predilection for a Tess made to seem real.

Irving Howe also appreciates the "real" Tess and he exonerates Hardy from a charge of molding his heroine to fit male preconceptions. Yet he himself indulges more freely in sexual generalizations than he is quite willing to admit Hardy does. After praising Tess's individuation by Hardy, Howe reminds us always to remember that "she is a woman." While claiming that Tess represents herself and not an idea, he all but counters the claim in the way he puts it: Hardy's purpose is "not to make her a goddess or a metaphor, it is to underscore her embattled womanliness." Here the critic, like the author on occasion, falls afoul of the generic implications of the word "woman."

Comparable tension between statement and implication appears in Jean Brooks's chapter on *Tess*. In her view, Hardy finds idealizing perception such as Angel's the projection of a "lifeless image," distorting, betraying, and entirely "inadequate." As evidence that Hardy condemns depersonalization, she cites the two harvesting scenes. One assimilates Tess to the machine she services—she loses independence of action or will. One assimilates her to the natural scene—she loses her margin and becomes a portion of the field. Brooks follows Hardy in disapproving of the first mode of assimilation and finding charm in the second, but fails to point out that *both* dissolve the margin of distinct personality. Brooks's preference for personalization over depersonalization begins to look like preference for one sort of depersonalization over another. In fact, in celebrating Tess's uniqueness, Brooks's own language stresses the heroine's womanhood in a way that transforms the individual woman into an abstraction: she praises Tess's "vibrant humanity, her woman's power of suffering, renewal, and compassion."

John Lucas and Rosalind Miles are two more critics who applaud Tess's effort to live as a fully real individual, while the conflicts found in the language they employ to express their view are especially striking. Lucas himself recognizes certain stereotypical and demeaning connotations of the phrase "a pure woman." Still, he goes ahead to use this phrase. He admires Tess's striving not to be fixed by images of purity and woman-hood, and actually points out the irony of the subtitle—it invokes one of the standardized identities men seek to pin on her. But in his admiration for Tess's individuality, he pins this identity on her himself: "Simply, Tess is a pure woman." Hard-beset by male-imposed labels, according to Lucas, she is determined to live "from some center, some awareness of herself as pure woman, purely a woman." Similarly, according to Miles, while Hardy gives Tess representative status, he never loses sight of her personal uniqueness, "as a woman, and a woman living in that time and place." It is strange but not unusual that she should cite in admiration of an indi-vidualized Tess the passage that describes her as a figure forming part of the landscape, "a field-woman pure and simple."

In covert re-introductions of gender generics into discussions of Tess even by those who declare Hardy's and their own respect for individuality, we see paradoxically dramatized the delight-giving, dangerous dialectic of knowledge that the novel is about. In fact, the subtitle of my own essay may seem correspondingly equivocal—because of the usage of the word "woman" in our language. But I mean to equivocate. "Hardy on Knowing a Woman" means "Hardy on Knowing a Woman as Individual and Sexual Abstraction." The way a woman is known reveals the complexity of knowing. That is, *Tess* invites but frustrates over-simplification. It is easy to say that Angel wrongs Tess by perceiving her not just as herself but as an essence and type of womanhood, harder to face the ultimate force of the fact that he also loves her because of it. So does Hardy. So do we, if he has his way. Object of desire and also aesthetic object as the preface hints, Tess as pure woman is beloved and beautiful, inspires love, inspires art by the same token that she suffers misapprehension and misuse. Finally she really does lose her margin, her life.

Hardy: "Full-Hearted Evensong"

Philip M. Weinstein

The simplest way to orient my commentary on *Tess of the D'Urbervilles* is to juxtapose it against Lionel Johnson's well-known stricture (at the conclusion of his study of Hardy):

> the world was very strong; her conscience was blinded and bewildered; she did some things nobly, and some despairingly: but there is nothing . . . to suggest that she was wholly an irresponsible victim of her own temperament, and of adverse circumstances. . . . Like Maggie Tulliver, Tess might have gone to Thomas à Kempis: one of the very few writers, whom experience does not prove untrue. She went through fire and water, and made no true use of them: she is pitiable, but not admirable.

These are cogent and thoughtful remarks, but they seem to me fundamentally amiss. The judgmental bias is strong in them, and that bias is one of immaculateness. "The world" is a place that one is meant to be superior to; Maggie Tulliver succeeded better than Tess at this task, and she is therefore "admirable." By positing Kempis-like self-transcendence as the model of the self, Johnson fails to see that *Tess* is a novel not of failed

---

From *The Semantics of Desire: Changing Models of Identity from Dickens to Joyce.* © 1984 by Princeton University Press.

transcendence but of tragically achieved immersion. Her violated virginity radiates this novel's values, just as Maggie's intact virginity radiates that novel's values. The kindred issue of virginity serves to emphasize the changes in setting, psychology, and plot that we find when we move from Eliot to Hardy. *Tess of the D'Urbervilles* is the story neither of a pure nor of an impure woman: it is the story of an *embodied* woman whose career cuts athwart and exposes transcendental notions of good and evil.

The world outside the self, as Eliot imagines it, resists the transforming moral energies of her protagonists, but it does not ultimately negate them. The wide-awake altruistic decency of figures like Adam Bede, Romola, Felix Holt, Mary Garth, and Daniel Deronda encounters grating setbacks but not defeat. Lydgate's "spots of commonness" are just that—local blemishes rather than cosmic ill—and they are reformable, if not eradicable. Thus one may say of Eliot's world what cannot be said of Hardy's: that the struggle of the moral life is its dominant concern, and that this struggle may in a significant measure succeed, when conducted with humility, sympathy, and a perseverance at once ardent and alert. Maggie and Gwendolen appear in this study because they are suggestive exceptions to the moral norm thus sketched out. What they suggest is that the career of ardent human energy is more wayward, more vulnerable to stresses within and without, than can be conveyed in the set of values through which Eliot chooses to read that career. The embodied behavior of Maggie and Gwendolen, as I have tried to show [elsewhere], means something other and more than Eliot is prepared to say.

In Hardy, by way of contrast, this failure of behavior to square with a paradigm of immaculate values is anything but a novelistic embarrassment: it is the enabling premise of his mature art. He has simply taken some salient characteristics of the nineteenth-century intellectual's view of the natural world—its infinitely gradated causality, its meaningless interpenetration of forces, its play of unsanctioned energy—and found them at work in the human world as well. As J. I. M. Stewart says, "What was felt as potentially subversive in Hardy was not his universe . . . but his predisposition to let his sense of that universe act, however cautiously, upon areas of experience hitherto fenced off because of the explosive material apprehended as buried there." This penetration of the natural into the human results in Hardy's showing us, supremely in *Tess*, "what the woman is— what she IS—inhumanly, physiologically, materially" [D. H. Lawrence quoted from *D. H. Lawrence: Selected Literary Criticism*]. More, he shows us this against the human background of what the woman poignantly wills herself to be. The tension within Tess between the "natural" and the "human" is the novel's characteristic note. As Angel tells his mother, with implications he himself is to suffer but never to grasp, "we are all children of the soil." It is a parentage as unsought and uncomfortable as it is inalienable. In Hardy's unsentimental world the soil is simply hostile to the projects of human consciousness. Successful adaptation occurs only at the end, in the consciousless repose of death.

Repose, the relaxation of a vigilant scrutiny: these are the morally charged terms in which Eliot invites us to evaluate Maggie's lapse with Stephen Guest. Johnson (and a host of critics after him) uses the same framework to judge Tess's lapse with Alec d'Urberville. The two scenes, however, are shaped to different purposes. A metaphoric lapsing in *The Mill on the Floss* is replaced in *Tess of the D'Urbervilles* by literal unconsciousness. Before her intercourse with Alec, Tess sinks into sleep, ringed round and penetrated by the conditions of maculate nature:

> She was silent, and the horse ambled along for a considerable distance, till a faint luminous fog, which had hung in the hollows all the evening, became general and enveloped them. . . . She was inexpressibly weary. . . . By this time the moon had quite gone down, and partly on account of the fog The Chase was wrapped in thick darkness, although morning was not far off. He was obliged to advance with outstretched hands to avoid contact with the boughs, and discovered that to hit the exact spot from which he had started was at first entirely beyond him. . . . "Tess!" said d'Urberville.
>
> There was no answer. The obscurity was now so great that he could see absolutely nothing but a pale nebulousness at his feet, which represented the white muslin figure he had left upon the dead leaves. Everything else was blackness alike. D'Urberville stooped; and heard a gentle regular breathing. He knelt and bent lower, till her breath warmed his face, and in a moment his cheek was in contact with hers. She was sleeping soundly, and upon her eyelashes there lingered tears.

Settings in Eliot often seem shaped to symbolize human situations. They exist as passive background, corroborating the potential behavior of the characters in the foreground. (One thinks of scenes like Maggie among the gypsies or her drifting on the water with Stephen, in *The Mill on the Floss*, and of the archery contest at the Arrowpoints' or Deronda rowing on the Thames, in *Daniel Deronda*.) The memorable settings in Hardy (like the one just quoted) rarely function in this way. Rather, the characters, with their relative dispositions, wander into and are penetrated, reshaped, by non-human nature, with its absolute disposition. The dark and foggy Chase minimizes the potency of individual will; the passage of time gradually enervates Tess's powers of resistance. Differences between Tess and Alec are dwarfed by the overarching and quietly penetrative medium that contains them both. Within this setting Tess's self-protective, self-distinguishing consciousness cedes control. Her bodily conditions reassert their primacy.

Prior to Hardy, sleep appears in English fiction mainly as a brief interlude between stretches of consciousness. Or it may function poetically as the vehicle of another form of consciousness, that of dreams which prophetically announce future events or reinterpret present ones. In Hardy, and *a fortiori* in Joyce, sleep acquires a measure of its daily weight. It begins to appear not only as the condition in which a rough third of life is passed, but as a revealing sidelight on the phenomenon of consciousness. Hardy's stress on sleep emphasizes the fragile and intermittent hold human beings maintain upon themselves, and it throws into relief those crises attendant upon a relaxation of identity.

The determining scenes in *Tess of the D'Urbervilles* are articulated in terms of sleep; and we can already see, in the one quoted, that the undoing of Tess is something other than simple rape. The softness, stillness, and drowsiness of the setting and its human figures do not permit such a restrictive interpretation of violent resistance (for without resistance there can be no rape). The encounter is best seen as an event poised between consciousness and unconsciousness, between human resistance and natural yielding. As Ian Gregor says, it is "both a seduction *and* a rape," for Alex is simultaneously everything and nothing to her, a man who violated her conscious will and yet retains the most intimate hold upon her in the measure that it was he who "brought to consciousness her own sexuality." Upon scrutiny "her own sexuality" becomes, in Hardy's rendering, a contradiction in terms. Sexuality appears as the incompatible crossing of private and common, human and natural. It is the dimension through which Tess becomes most profoundly her own self and yet nature's plaything; and Hardy's genius, in this decisive scene, is to saturate her identity-bearing encounter in the unindividualized unconsciousness of sleep. We are made to take it as neither her act nor her accident, but instead an event that defines *in nuce* that openness to context which is Tess's authentic mode of response, while yet bearing no part in her conscious identity.

Another passage, this one during Angel's courtship, may shed more light on the extraordinary perspective Hardy maintains upon his heroine:

She had not heard him enter, and hardly realized his presence there. She was yawning, and he saw the red interior of her mouth as if it had been a snake's. She had stretched one arm so high above her coiled-up cable of hair that he could see its satin delicacy above the sunburn; her face was flushed with sleep, and her eyelids hung heavy over their pupils.

Need it be said that Eliot does not grasp her people at these moments—before they have "become themselves"? Hardy has an uncanny capacity to render the Tess that exists, incarnate, unthinking, behind "Tess." He gives us here the Tess who is the ground of "Tess." Her bodily gestures are unconscious, massive, lovingly described. The Tess Durbeyfield whom Angel Clare involuntarily falls in love with—though not the one he argues with—is in the main this pre-conscious physical presence. And the Tess Durbeyfield who slays Alec at the end is the same immediate creature; her impact on others and her receipt of their impact are essentially instinctive. (I hope that the reader will not misconstrue this approach to Tess (either Hardy's or mine) as an "excessively male" and narrow-minded focus on her body. It seems to me that Hardy attends to her dual being—as an incarnate woman subjectively known from within and objectively approached from outside—with perfect seriousness and artistic integrity. [By contrast Alec and Angel appear to be more cursory creations, realized by means of broader brush strokes.] In the framework of my own study, I would emphasize that Tess's "physical career" is under scrutiny in the same way that David's and Maggie's were earlier, and that Stephen's and Bloom's and Molly's will be later. The issue is not male/female but immaculate/incarnate.)

The scene at Stonehenge of her arrest for that act contains Hardy's final description of Tess asleep:

In a minute or two her breathing became more regular, her clasp of his hand relaxed, and she fell asleep. . . . Presently the night wind died out, and the quivering little pools in the cup-like hollows of the stones lay still. At the same time something seemed to move on the verge of the dip eastward—a mere dot. It was the head of a man approaching them. . . . "It is no use, sir," he said. "There are sixteen of us on the Plain, and the whole country is reared."

"Let her finish her sleep!" he [Angel] implored in a whisper of the men as they gathered round.

When they saw where she lay, which they had not done till

then, they showed no objection, and stood watching her, as still as the pillars around. He went to the stone and bent over her, holding one poor little hand; her breathing now was quick and small, like that of a lesser creature than a woman. All waited in the growing light. . . . Soon the light was strong, and a ray shone upon her unconscious form, peering under her eyelids and waking her.

"What is it, Angel?" she said, starting up. "Have they come for me?"

"Yes, dearest," he said. "They have come."

"It is as it should be," she murmured.

The scene of seizure is as measured and surprisingly gentle as the earlier one of violation. The law, for this rapt moment, waits upon the breath and pulse of a sleeping woman, taking her natural rhythms as a guide for its own pace: Hardy deliberately lengthens out the process of her awakening. Tess appears for the last time as the creature of sleep, obedient to stresses outside her own consciousness. She entered the concatenation of tragic events by falling asleep in a cart, and she leaves it after a brief respite of self-recomposing slumber atop an oblong slab at Stonehenge. The tension between human and natural will soon be stilled. "I am ready," she says.

This image of seventeen men waiting upon the pulse of one woman is more than picturesque; it suggests Hardy's underlying measure for assessing behavior. The clue to human actions lies less in conceptualized principles than in deeply rooted impulses. Moral assessment becomes authentic on condition that it descend to the earth in continuous recognition of the individual creature's incarnate, involuntary pulse beat. For the unsentimental Hardy, impulse may be no model for morality, but no morality that scorns impulse can be effective. Hortatory and high-minded models of behavior fail insofar as they ignore the embodied conditions of the creatures they would elevate.

In an exceedingly ironic passage Hardy has Angel Clare make just such a discovery:

He held that education had as yet but little affected the beats of emotion and impulse on which domestic happiness depends. It was probable that . . . improved systems of moral and intellectual training would appreciably, perhaps considerably, elevate the involuntary and even the unconscious instincts of human nature; but up to the present day culture, as far as he could see, might be said to have affected only the mental epiderm of those lives which had been brought under its influence.

The irony is that Angel is more the victim than the master of this insight. He is moved decisively by "beats of emotion and impulse" that are foreign to the "improved systems of moral and intellectual training" that he would call his principles. Beneath these principles, at a level of emotion and impulse he has no access to, Angel rages irrationally at Tess, able neither to forgive her nor to cease loving her. He remains blank to these depths, however, professing to live on a plane of rational magnanimity and detachment.

His utterances to Tess are suffused with unacknowledged resentment:

"But do not make me reproach you. I have sworn that I will not; and I will do everything to avoid it."

"Don't, Tess; don't argue. Different societies, different manners. You almost make me say you are an unapprehending peasant woman, who have never been initiated into the proportions of social things."

"My position—is this. . . . I thought—any man would have thought—that by giving up all ambition to win a wife with social standing, with fortune, with knowledge of the world, I should secure rustic innocence as surely as I should secure pink cheeks; but—However, I am no man to reproach you, and I will not."

The candor of Tess appears nowhere else in Hardy's fiction, but the duplicity of Angel is writ large in the obscurities of Jude and Sue. Repressing the outrage of his involuntary impulses, denying his anger, Angel passes off his bile —as the gentler Jude will later—under the banner of magnanimity. "You almost make me say" indeed! He can reproach her only by denying that he does so; he can abandon her only by proclaiming that "There is no anger between us."

As sleep indicates the integration of Tess with her natural conditions, so sleep reveals the double truth of Angel's emotional torment:

Clare came close, and bent over her. "Dead, dead, dead!" he murmured.

After fixedly regarding her for some moments with the same gaze of immeasurable woe he bent lower, enclosed her in his arms, and rolled her in the sheet as in a shroud. Then lifting her

> from the bed with as much respect as one would show to a dead
> body, he carried her across the room, murmuring—
>   "My poor, poor Tess—my dearest, darling Tess! So sweet, so
> good, so true! . . . My wife—dead, dead!" he said.

The conflict between traditional and Freudian readings of this scene is only apparent. It is as true that Clare's principles must be put to sleep before his deeper tenderness for her can emerge, as it is true that at the outraged core of his being he wants her to die. Freud has noted drily in "The Ego and the Id" that "the normal man is not only far more immoral than he believes but also far more moral than he knows." Correspondingly, Angel Clare loves and hates Tess Durbeyfield with an intensity of which he is wholly unconscious. Could he find access to this level, he might vent his fury and recover his buried affection. Instead, he proclaims his behavior to be rational and detached: an affair of the immaculate spirit fulfilling itself in irreproachable conduct. He has yet to learn that life in Hardy, including his own, has no transcendental sanction, but is instead a process of pulsation and interpenetration.

Tess, by contrast with Angel's doubleness, is essentially (often helplessly) attuned to the deeper pulse within and about her. The poetry of this novel consists in Hardy's evocation of the shared pulsebeat connecting the human Tess with her natural matrix:

> She did not know that Clare had followed her round, and that
> he sat under his cow watching her. The stillness of her head and
> features was remarkable: she might have been in a trance, her
> eyes open, yet unseeing. Nothing in the picture moved but Old
> Pretty's tail and Tess's pink hands, the latter so gently as to be a
> rhythmic pulsation only, as if they were obeying a reflex stimu-
> lus, like a beating heart.

This is the inconceivable motion of process itself, of "earth's diurnal course"; Hardy shares something of Wordsworth's capacity to make perceptible the infinitesimal movement of momentary life. It is idle to read Tess's trance-like state as a regrettable and ominous lapse of attention. Such criticism mistakenly sees her as failing the dictates of a paradigm of immaculateness, rather than fulfilling the conditions of a paradigm of immersion. The terrible beauty of Tess is that she is so unquestionably bodily, penetrable. Hardy never shows her but as, literally, a figure of flesh and blood, colored by what she moves against, with a quicksilver pulse:

They were breaking up the masses of curd before putting them into the vats . . . and amid the immaculate whiteness of the curds Tess Durbeyfield's hands showed themselves of the pinkness of the rose. Angel, who was filling the vats with his handfuls, suddenly ceased, and laid his hands flat upon hers. Her sleeves were rolled far above the elbow, and bending lower he kissed the inside vein of her soft arm.

Although the early September weather was sultry, her arm, from her dabbling in the curds, was as cold and damp to his mouth as a new-gathered mushroom, and tasted of the whey. But she was such a sheaf of susceptibilities that her pulse was accelerated by the touch, her blood driven to her finger-ends, and the cool arms flushed hot.

The patient physical detail is exquisite; and it shows, among other things, that curds, mushroom, whey, and hands differ in degree only, not in kind. They are all part of the material bounty of nature, a "new gathered" joy for the appetite, to be relished now in their fluid and susceptible ripeness. Such a passage brings home the conviction that in this novel Hardy's imagined world has, as its center, not a disembodied law but a beating heart. There is in *Tess of the D'Urbervilles* plenty (indeed, overmuch) of talk about laws, but deeper than Logos is pulsation. To approach the core of Tess is to move her blood, as Angel does lovingly here. To destroy another is to puncture his heart and stop his pulse: Prince and Alec die through eruption of heart blood. Because pulsation is a rhythm so suffused throughout the novel as to appear its natural law, one accepts as a statement of irresistible process Hardy's words:

In reality, she was drifting into acquiescence. Every see-saw of her breath, every wave of her blood, every pulse singing in her ears, was a voice that joined with nature in revolt against her scrupulousness.

"Drifting . . . see-saw . . . wave . . . pulse"—these words convey the gentle sway of nature upon the human. That sway is more darkly described in the language of disfigurement and abrasion. I have already glanced at the crucial instances of penetration—the wounding of Prince, the seduction of Tess, the murder of Alec—and those scenes survive their tincture of melodrama mainly because they are couched upon innumerable humbler instances of the same dynamic. The much-discussed scene in the garden—Tess "gathering cuckoo-spittle on her skirts, cracking snails that were underfoot, staining her hands with thistle-milk and slug-slime"—dramatizes the same process. To move toward Clare is to brush against and become stained by the foul and fecund low-life that fills Hardy's landscape. Margaret Drabble remarks, in an essay on "Hardy and the Natural World," that "oddly enough, the vegetative blemishes [of nature] seem to have upset and preyed on his mind more than the more obvious signs of nature's cruelty." "Upset" is perhaps the wrong verb. Hardy's stance in these descriptions is as often neutral, even celebratory, as it is disturbed. He seems to have visually apprehended in nature less its hostility than its indifference and its inhuman commerce. (Hardy's natural world, as Tanner and others have noticed, has its emptiness as well as its commerce, perhaps most stunningly rendered in the scene of Tess and Marian in the swede-field at Flintcomb-Ash. More typically, I believe, emptiness is Hardy's *idea* of a nature that knows us not. His actual descriptions are lovingly stocked with instances of its manifold and inhuman vitality.)

The following passage, for example, could be penned by no one else:

> Their gauzy skirts had brushed up from the grass innumerable
> flies and butterflies which, unable to escape, remained caged in
> the transparent tissue as in an aviary.

A writer who can see these flies—and elsewhere it is pollen, peat, lichen, algae, scrub plants, caterpillars, and moths—is not likely to take virginity of any sort seriously. The world he imaginatively inhabits is no discarnate vacuum for the transcendental spirit but a material plenitude, teeming with all strata of living creatures, marked by ineradicable stain, humming with cross-pollenization. He who never liked to be touched knows that we are forced to share the scene: that, in life, human bodies are touched by non-human bodies, and in death devoured by them.

For Tess to be shown in nature means, then, to be shown in an embrace that increasingly erodes her human personality. The embrace is beautiful to the onlooker but eventually abrasive and disfiguring to the subject. Consider her binding the corn:

> Her binding proceeds with clock-like monotony. From the
> sheaf last finished she draws a handful of ears, patting their tips
> with her left palm to bring them even. Then stooping low she
> moves forward, gathering the corn with both hands against her
> knees, and pushing her left gloved hand under the bundle to
> meet the right on the other side, holding the corn in an embrace

like that of a lover. She brings the ends of the bond together, and kneels on the sheaf while she ties it, beating back her skirts now and then when lifted by the breeze. A bit of her naked arm is visible between the buff leather of the gauntlet and the sleeve of her gown; and as the day wears on its feminine smoothness becomes scarified by the stubble, and bleeds.

The passage is almost beyond commentary. In an eternal present tense (to which Hardy recurs) her way of working, her way of feeling, her sexual bond to the earth (its child, its lover), and the effects of that bond upon her (its victim) are seamlessly fused. Hardy renders both the otherness of the earth—its different substance, detail by detail, from her own substance—and the kinship of the earth—her sustained embrace of its produce. Her movement is so rhythmic and habitual as to be half trance-like. It both exhausts her and defines, in something like the following terms, her commerce with nature: a commerce that is involuntary, bodily, and continuous, that becomes loverly and abrasive as it is prolonged, that leads to bleeding and ultimately (by implication) to death.

Perhaps the richest concentration of this cluster of meanings occurs in the treacle scene with Car Darch:

> "Well—whatever is that a-creeping down thy back, Car Darch?" said one of the group suddenly.
>
> All looked at Car. Her gown was a light cotton print, and from the back of her head a kind of rope could be seen descending to some distance below her waist, like a Chinaman's queue.
>
> "Tis her hair falling down," said another.
>
> No; it was not her hair: it was black stream of something oozing from her basket, and it glistened like a slimy snake in the cold still rays of the moon.
>
> "Tis treacle," said an observant matron.
>
> Treacle it was. Car's poor old grandmother had a weakness for the sweet stuff. Honey she had in plenty out of her own hives, but treacle was what her soul desired, and Car had been about to give her a treat of surprise. Hastily lowering the basket the dark girl found that the vessel containing the syrup had been smashed within.
>
> By this time there had arisen a shout of laughter at the extraordinary appearance of Car's back, which irritated the dark queen into getting rid of the disfigurement by the first sudden

means available, and independently of the help of the scoffers. She rushed excitedly into the field they were about to cross, and flinging herself flat on her back upon the grass, began to wipe her gown as well as she could by spinning horizontally on the herbage and dragging herself over it upon her elbows.

The scene is surrounded by others that are just as sexually laden—the "vegeto-human pollen" of the Dionysiac dancers before and the finely penetrating mist of the violation scene after. Here the suggested visual meanings are most portentous, though: like blood or semen, the oozing treacle disfigures the female whom it stains, descending down her back "to some distance below her waist," glistening "like a slimy snake." If the serpent simile conveys the evil of sexuality, yet the treacle is intrinsically delicious and life-sustaining. Its connection with honey and hives brings Tess's ill-fated trip with Prince to mind; and here, as there, the image powerfully coalesces richness and violation: "the vessel containing the syrup had been smashed within." It takes violation to release richness, and the life-stuff—blood, semen, treacle—flows out, staining and deforming what it touches, bringing ecstasy or violence as its consequences. Car Darch, trying to rid herself of the treacle, writhes on the grass as though in the throes of sexual frenzy. In a moment she will seek to punish Tess physically for having stolen her lover, and will thus catapult her into Alec's arms. With its tumult and its ritual beauty, its drunkenness and prolific waste of sweetness, its disregard for individual preferences, such a scene conveys, in lyrical epitome, the Schopenhauerian ordeal that Hardy envisaged as the plight of human beings, caught up in the unsought stresses of inhuman nature.

What is the effect of such a world upon the human beings who suffer it? Can the human assimilate the natural and remain human? Before assessing Tess's final stance, one needs to note that the pantheistic solution of amoral merging with natural forces is possible only for Hardy's coarser characters, those with a less individualized consciousness. Tess's parents may drift into a drunken haze of painlessness, Car Darch and her friends may see "themselves and surrounding nature [as] forming an organism of which all the parts harmoniously and joyously interpenetrated each other." But Tess is condemned—like all of Hardy's reflective people—to absorb the impress of nature's inhuman otherness. Not harmonious merging but sustained abrasion is her portion: "She lay in a state of percipience without volition, and the rustle of the straw and the cutting of the [corn] ears by the others had the weight of bodily touches."

The final effect of accumulating experience upon the human organism is something like an overwhelming. Despite his awareness of the circulating blood and its restorative flow, Hardy permits his protagonists little psychological capacity for assimilation: they are unable to *get done* with anything. They forget nothing, nor do those who can make them suffer ever disappear. The cycle of fermenting nature around and within them is silhouetted against the echoing stasis of Hardy's gaunt, unchanging geography and cast of characters. Because nature is cyclical and memoryless, Tess physically blooms again, but it is only nature in her that is fully recovered and blooming. Humanly, as opposed to naturally, she is moving in an irreversible linear direction. What appears to her in its early stages as "a liberal education" will eventually, inevitably, be perceived as an absurd "sport."

This tension in Tess between nature that meaninglessly renews itself and humanity that ages and darkens wisely is held, until the end, in precarious balance. Tess is, as it were, "layered" in time, speaking both dialect and standard English, containing still "her twelfth year in her cheeks . . . her ninth sparkling from her eyes, and even her fifth" now and then in "the curves of her mouth," emerging as a composite of Christian and pagan, Victorian and Jacobean, Durbeyfield and d'Urberville. Her time-enriched, culturally crossed identity contains a mixture of elements whose range neither she nor Angel can grasp—she wanting to believe that she is unchanged, he that she is all changed. Both refer to a partial entity named "Tess," whereas Hardy shows us the wholeness of an embodied Tess—what the woman is, as well as what she feels—a wholeness that alters in time and yet remains (to us, not—finally—to her) recognizably one. For the worst breach that Tess suffers is the severance of Tess from "Tess": the inability, after her last experience with Alec, to keep her moral idea of herself and her felt awareness of her own body any longer together: "But he had a vague consciousness of one thing, though it was not clear to him till later; that his original Tess had spiritually ceased to recognize the body before him as hers—allowing it to drift, like a corpse upon the current, in a direction dissociated from its living will."

In a novel that is unfailingly sagacious, this insight is perhaps supreme. The fate of being embodied, of being a child of the soil, has so violated Tess's transcendental image of herself as immaculate and unchanged, as still Angel's, that her mind, in a paroxysm of guilt, has snapped away from its container of estranging dross. In the mid-twentieth century R. D. Laing writes cogently about "the divided self," but Hardy's contemporary reviewers could have done little with this perception. Andrew Lang protests:

"She does not die, like Clarissa . . . but she goes back to the atrocious cad who betrayed her, and wears—not caring what she wears—the parasol of pomp and the pretty slippers of iniquity." Annoyed by Tess's flashy clothes, Lang is asking her to recover from her moral lapse at least to the extent of feeling and expressing guilt. He does not see that Hardy is dramatizing, in Tess's torpor, not a deficiency but an excess of guilt: indeed, a kind of temporary insanity that transpires when the spiritual insistence on immaculate self-definition abrades once too often against the indifferent moral facts of embodied life. The identity of "Tess" can no longer sustain the incarnate career of Tess. Humanity and nature are irreconcilable in the same human being: the outraged soul disowns the body, ceding it and its apparel to Alec.

If you are small enough, in Hardy's world, you can retain civil relations between soul and body, and this unaspiring civility marks the charm of Hardy's rustics. His Prometheans, however, those who make demands on life, regularly collapse upon themselves, their human project exploded by the forces of nature within and without. As J. Hillis Miller says, Hardy responds to this collapse less by questioning the human project that has collapsed than by quarreling with the immovable natural obstacle. Hardy bemoans the inevitability of failure, rather than asking what change in human values might permit success. "Like so many of his countrymen, like Dickens for example," Miller writes, "he fears the guilt involved in becoming the value-giving center of his world." If one grants the menacing contours of Hardy's natural world, then this fear simply guarantees the miscarriage of human aspiration. Penetrated through and through with nature, we are what we are; Hardy knows this, and he knows that this is not what we would be. He cannot rise to Nietzsche's audacious counsel to redefine therefore what we would be: "You shall become who you are."

As a result there are few moments of crisis overcome in Hardy's novels—moments when the natural, having invaded the human, finds itself assimilated and humanized. Two such moments, though, can be found in *Tess of the D'Urbervilles*. The first in Tess's burial of her child Sorrow. Rising into godlike authority, generating the terms of good and evil out of her own bodily travail, Tess baptizes her child and buries it "in that shabby corner of God's allotment where he lets the nettles grow, and where all unbaptized infants, notorious drunkards, suicides, and others of the conjecturally damned are laid." The second moment of serenity is the "fulfillment" of Phase the Seventh, Tess reunited with Angel. Beyond expectation, she is finally beyond pain; relinquishment of the future permits the past to subside. Having taken in Alec to the full, she now has seven indescribable days with Angel. "This happiness could not have lasted," she rightly says, for duration and fulfillment are conflicting notions in Hardy's world.

Rather than fulfillment, then, let us call it penetration, absolute yielding. This is a novel about living richness, about the release, despoliation, and exhaustion of human resource. Tess is ready to die because she has given and taken as much as a human being can give and take. Like those prime milchers whose excess of liquid "oozed forth and fell in drops," Tess is recurrently described with "drops upon her hair, like seed pearls." Living things exist here to be penetrated and to pass on their very last drop of sweetness to other living things. "Songs were often resorted to in dairies hereabout as an enticement to the cows when they showed signs of withholding their usual yield." The song is *Tess*.

Chronology

1840	Thomas Hardy is born on June 2 in Higher Bockhampton, a community in the parish of Stinsford, Dorset. He is the son of Thomas Hardy, a stonemason, and Jemima Hand Hardy.
1848	Begins his education at a school in Lower Bockhampton.
1849	Hardy is transferred to a school in Dorchester.
1855	Begins teaching at the Stinsford Church Sunday School.
1856	Hardy is accepted at the office of architect John Hicks as a pupil. Also in this year Hardy meets Horace Moule and William Barnes.
ca. 1860	Hardy writes his first poem, called "Domicilium."
1862	After settling in London, Hardy goes to work for architect and church restorer Arthur Blomfield. He reads widely, studies paintings at the National Gallery, and becomes an agnostic.
1863	The Royal Institute of British Architects awards Hardy an essay prize.
1865	*Chambers' Journal* publishes "How I Built Myself a House." Hardy attends French classes at King's College, Cambridge.
1867	Hardy returns to Dorset and resumes working for John Hicks. At this time, however, he also begins work on his first novel, *The Poor Man and the Lady*.
1868	*The Poor Man and the Lady* is rejected by Macmillan; Hardy resubmits the manuscript to Chapman & Hall.
1869	Hardy meets George Meredith. Begins his second novel, *Desperate Remedies*.
1870	Hardy travels to Cornwall, where he meets Emma Lavinia Gifford, his future wife. Publisher William Tinsley agrees to produce *Desperate Remedies* at the author's expense.
1871	*Desperate Remedies* is published. Also in this year Hardy writes *Under the Greenwood Tree* and begins *A Pair of Blue Eyes*.

1872 *Under the Greenwood Tree* is published; *A Pair of Blue Eyes* appears in serial form.

1873 Hardy's friend Horace Moule commits suicide. Hardy is invited by Leslie Stephen to contribute to *Cornhill*; Hardy then begins the serialized version of *Far from the Madding Crowd*. *A Pair of Blue Eyes* is published.

1874 *Far from the Madding Crowd* is published. Hardy marries Emma Lavinia Gifford; they travel to France after the wedding, and upon return settle in Surbiton.

1876 *The Hand of Ethelberta* appears. Hardy and his wife travel to Holland and Germany, and then move to a home at Sturminster Newton, in Dorset.

1878 *The Return of the Native* is published. Hardy moves once again, to London, where he is elected to the Savile Club.

1879 Hardy pursues research for *The Trumpet-Major* in the British Museum.

1880 *The Trumpet-Major* is published. Hardy meets the Poet Laureate, Alfred, Lord Tennyson. The writing of *A Laodicean* is slowed by a serious illness.

1881 *A Laodicean* is published.

1882 *Two on a Tower* is published.

1883 Hardy moves to Dorchester where he begins building his home, Max Gate. "The Dorsetshire Labourer" appears in *Longman's Magazine*.

1884 Hardy begins composition of *The Mayor of Casterbridge*.

1885 Moves into Max Gate. He starts writing *The Woodlanders*.

1886 *The Mayor of Casterbridge* is published.

1887 *The Woodlanders* is published. Hardy visits Italy.

1888 *The Wessex Tales*, a collection of short stories, is published. Composition of *Tess of the D'Urbervilles* begins.

1889 Several publishers reject the first installments of *Tess*.

1890 Hardy finishes *Tess*.

1891 Both *Tess of the D'Urbervilles* and *A Group of Noble Dames* are published.

1892 Hardy's father dies. The first version of *The Well-Beloved* is serialized. Relations with his wife begin to deteriorate and worsen over the next two years, particularly during the composition of *Jude the Obscure*.

1893 Hardy travels to Dublin and Oxford, where he visits Florence Henniker, with whom he writes a short story, and, it is believed, falls in love.

1894   *Life's Little Ironies*, a collection of poems, is published.

1895   *Jude the Obscure* is published and receives primarily outraged reviews. As a result Hardy decides to discontinue novel-writing and henceforward produces only poetry. Also in this year Hardy works on the Uniform Edition of his novels.

1897   *The Well-Beloved* is published.

1898   Publishes *The Wessex Poems*.

1901   Publishes *Poems of the Past and the Present*.

1904   *The Dynasts*, part 1, is published. Hardy's mother dies.

1905   Hardy receives an honorary LL.D. from Aberdeen.

1906   *The Dynasts*, part 2, is published.

1908   *The Dynasts*, part 3, is published.

1909   Publishes *Time's Laughingstocks*. Hardy becomes the governor of the Dorchester Grammar School.

1910   Hardy is awarded the O.M. (Order of Merit).

1912   Hardy's wife Emma Lavinia dies on November 27.

1913   *A Changed Man* is published. Hardy receives an honorary D.Litt. degree from Cambridge; he is also made an honorary Fellow of Magdalen College, Cambridge.

1914   Hardy marries Florence Emily Dugdale. The collection of poems called *Satires of Circumstance* is published. As World War I begins Hardy joins a group of writers dedicated to the support of the Allied cause.

1915   Hardy's sister Mary dies.

1917   *Moments of Vision*, a collection of poetry, is published.

1919   Hardy's first *Collected Poems* is published.

1920   Oxford University awards Hardy an honorary D.Litt.

1921   Publishes *Late Lyrics and Earlier*. Becomes honorary Fellow at Queen's College, Oxford.

1923   *The Famous Tragedy of the Queen of Cornwall* is published. Hardy receives a visit from the Prince of Wales at Max Gate.

1925   *Human Shows* is published.

1928   Hardy dies on January 11; his ashes are buried at Westminster Abbey, and his heart is placed at his first wife's grave in the Stinsford churchyard. *Winter Words* published posthumously. Florence Emily Hardy publishes *The Early Life of Thomas Hardy*, believed to have been written largely by Hardy himself.

1930   *Collected Poems* published posthumously. Florence Emily Hardy publishes *The Later Years of Thomas Hardy*.

Contributors

HAROLD BLOOM, Sterling Professor of the Humanities at Yale University, is the author of *The Anxiety of Influence*, *Poetry and Repression*, and many other volumes of literary criticism. His forthcoming study, *Freud: Transference and Authority*, attempts a full-scale reading of all of Freud's major writings. A MacArthur Prize Fellow, he is general editor of five series of literary criticism published by Chelsea House.

TONY TANNER is Reader in English at Cambridge University. His books include *The Reign of Wonder*, *City of Words*, and *Adultery in the Novel*.

BRUCE JOHNSON is Professor of English at the University of Rochester. He has written on Conrad and on Hardy; his most recent book is *True Correspondence: A Phenomenology of Thomas Hardy's Novels*.

MARY JACOBUS is Professor of English at Cornell University. She is author of *Tradition and Experiment in Wordsworth's Lyrical Ballads* and editor of *Women Writing and Writing About Women*.

J. HILLIS MILLER is Frederick W. Hilles Professor of English and Comparative Literature at Yale University. His books of criticism include *Poetry of Reality: Six Twentieth-Century Writers*, *Fiction and Repetition: Seven English Novels*, and *The Linguistic Moment: From Wordsworth to Stevens*.

KATHLEEN BLAKE is Professor of English at the University of Washington in Seattle. Her publications include *Love and the Woman Question in Victorian Literature: The Art of Self-Postponement* and *Play, Games, and Sport: The Literary Works of Lewis Carroll*.

PHILIP M. WEINSTEIN teaches at Swarthmore College. His most recent book is *The Semantics of Desire: The Changing Roles of Identity from Dickens to Joyce*.

Bibliography

Abercrombie, Lascelles. *Thomas Hardy: A Critical Study*. London: Martin Secker, 1912.

Alcorn, John. *The Nature Novel from Hardy to Lawrence*. New York: Columbia University Press, 1977.

Allen, Walter. *The English Novel*. London: Phoenix House, 1954.

Bayley, John. *An Essay on Hardy*. Cambridge: Cambridge University Press, 1978.

Beach, Joseph Warren. *The Technique of Thomas Hardy*. Chicago: The University of Chicago Press, 1922.

Bonica, Charlotte. "Nature and Paganism in Hardy's *Tess of the D'Urbervilles*." *ELH* 49, no. 4 (1982): 849–62.

Boumelha, Penny. *Thomas Hardy and Women: Sexual Ideology and Narrative Form*. Brighton, Sussex: The Harvester Press, 1982.

Brick, Allen. "Paradise and Consciousness in Hardy's *Tess*." *Nineteenth-Century Fiction* 17 (1962): 115–34.

Brooks, Jean R. "*Tess of the D'Urbervilles*: The Move Towards Existentialism." In *Thomas Hardy and the Modern World: Papers Presented at the 1973 Summer School*, edited by F. B. Pinion. Dorchester, Dorset: The Thomas Hardy Society, 1974.

———. *Thomas Hardy: The Poetic Structure*. Ithaca: Cornell University Press, 1971.

Brown, Suzanne Hunter. "'Tess' and *Tess*: An Experiment in Genre." *Modern Fiction Studies* 28 (1982): 25–44.

Carpenter, Richard. *Thomas Hardy*. New York: Twayne Publishers, 1964.

Casagrande, Peter J. *Unity in Hardy's Novels*. Lawrence, Kans.: The Regents Press of Kansas, 1982.

Cecil, David. *Hardy the Novelist*. New York: The Bobbs-Merrill Co., 1946.

Chew, Samuel C. *Thomas Hardy: Poet and Novelist*. 2d revision. New York: Russell & Russell, 1964.

Childers, Mary. "Thomas Hardy, the Man Who 'Liked' Women." *Criticism* 23, no. 4 (1981): 317–34.

Cox, R. G. *Thomas Hardy: The Critical Heritage*. London: Routledge & Kegan Paul, 1970.

Daiches, David. *Some Late Victorian Attitudes*. New York: W. W. Norton & Co., 1969.

De Laura, David J. "'The Ache of Modernism' in Hardy's Later Novels." *ELH* 34, no. 3 (1967): 380–99.

Draper, Ronald P., ed. *Hardy: The Tragic Novels: A Casebook*. London: Macmillan, 1975.

Edwards, Duane. "Chance in Hardy's Fiction." *Midwest Quarterly* 11 (1970): 427–41.

Egan, Joseph J. "The Fatal Suitor: Early Foreshadowings in *Tess of the D'Urbervilles*." *Tennessee Studies in Literature* 15 (1970): 161–64.

Elledge, Scott, ed. *Thomas Hardy*: Tess of the D'Urbervilles. A Norton Critical Edition. 2d ed. New York: W. W. Norton and Co., 1979.

Emmet, V. J., Jr. "Marriage in Hardy's Later Novels." *Midwest Quarterly* 10 (1969): 331–48.

Firor, Ruth A. *Folkways in Thomas Hardy*. Philadelphia: University of Pennsylvania Press, 1931.

Furbank, P. N. "Introduction." In *Tess of the D'Urbervilles*. The New Wessex Edition. London: Macmillan, 1975.

Gose, Elliott B., Jr. "Psychic Evolution: Darwinism and Initiation in *Tess of the D'Urbervilles*." *Nineteenth-Century Fiction* 18 (1963): 261–72.

Guerard, Albert J. *Thomas Hardy: The Novels and Stories*. Cambridge: Harvard University Press, 1949.

————, ed. *Hardy: A Collection of Critical Essays*. Englewood Cliffs, N. J.: Prentice-Hall, 1963.

Hall, W. F. "Hawthorne, Shakespeare and Tess: Hardy's Use of Allusion and Reference." *English Studies* 52 (1971): 533–42.

Hardy, Barbara. *Forms of Feeling in Victorian Fiction*. London: Peter Owen, 1985.

Hardy, Evelyn. *Thomas Hardy: A Critical Biography*. London: Hogarth Press, 1954.

Hardy, Florence Emily. *The Life of Thomas Hardy, 1840–1928*. London: Macmillan, 1962. Reprint. Hamden, Conn.: Shoe String Press, 1970.

Hazen, James. "Angel's Hellenism in *Tess of the D'Urbervilles*." *College Literature* 4 (1977): 129–35.

Herbert, Lucille. "Hardy's Views in *Tess of the D'Urbervilles*." *ELH* 37, no. 1 (1970): 77–94.

Hinde, Thomas. "Accident and Coincidence in *Tess of the D'Urbervilles*." In *The Genius of Thomas Hardy*, edited by Margaret Drabble, 74–79. New York: Alfred A. Knopf, 1976.

Hornback, Bert A. *The Metaphor of Chance: Vision and Technique in the Works of Thomas Hardy*. Athens: Ohio University Press, 1971.

Horne, Lewis B. "The Darkening Sun of Tess Durbeyfield." *Texas Studies in Literature and Language* 13 (1970): 299–311.

Howe, Irving. *Thomas Hardy*. New York: Macmillan, 1967.

Johnson, Bruce. *True Correspondence: A Phenomenology of Thomas Hardy's Novels*. Tallahassee: University Presses of Florida, 1983.

Johnson, Lionel. *The Art of Thomas Hardy*. New York: Russell & Russell, 1965.

Kozicki, Henry. "Myths of Redemption in Hardy's *Tess of the D'Urbervilles*." *Papers on Language and Literature* 10 (1974): 150–58.

Kramer, Dale. *Thomas Hardy: The Forms of Tragedy*. Detroit: Wayne State University Press, 1975.

Laird, J. T. *The Shaping of* Tess of the D'Urbervilles. Oxford: Oxford University Press, 1975.

————. "New Light on the Evolution of *Tess of the D'Urbervilles*." *Review of English Studies* 31, no. 124 (1980): 414–35.

LaValley, Albert J. *Twentieth Century Interpretations of* Tess of the D'Urbervilles: *A Collection of Critical Essays*. Englewood Cliffs, N. J.: Prentice-Hall, 1969.

Lawrence, D. H. *Phoenix: The Posthumous Papers of D. H. Lawrence*. New York: The Viking Press, 1972.

Lodge, David. "Tess, Nature and the Voices of Hardy." In *Language of Fiction: Essays in Criticism and Verbal Analysis of the English Novel*. London: Routledge & Kegan Paul, 1967.

Lucas, John. "Hardy's Women." In *The Literature of Change: Studies in the Nineteenth Century Provincial Novel*, 2d. ed., 119–91. Brighton, Sussex: The Harvester Press, 1980.

Millgate, Michael. *Thomas Hardy: A Biography*. New York: Random House, 1982.

———. *Thomas Hardy: His Career as a Novelist*. New York: Random House, 1971.

Millgate, Michael, and Richard Little Purdy, eds. *The Collected Letters of Thomas Hardy*. 3 volumes to date. Oxford: Oxford University Press, 1978–.

Morrell, Roy. *Thomas Hardy: The Will and the Way*. Kuala Lumpur: University of Malaya Press, 1968.

Page, Norman, ed. *Thomas Hardy: The Writer and His Background*. London: Bell & Hyman, 1980.

Pinion, F. B., ed. *A Hardy Companion: A Guide to the Works of Thomas Hardy and Their Background*. New York: St. Martin's Press, 1968.

Poole, Adrian. "Men's Words and Hardy's Women." *Essays in Criticism* 31, no. 4 (1981): 328–45.

Schweik, Robert C. "Moral Perspective in *Tess of the D'Urbervilles*." *College English* 24 (1962): 14–18.

Sherman, G. W. *The Pessimism of Thomas Hardy*. Rutherford, N. J.: Fairleigh Dickinson University Press, 1976.

Starzyk, Lawrence J. "The Coming Universal Wish Not to Live in Hardy's 'Modern' Novels." *Nineteenth-Century Fiction* 26 (1972): 419–35.

Thompson, Charlotte. "Language and the Shape of Reality in *Tess*." *ELH* 50, no. 4 (1983): 729–62.

Thurley, Geoffrey. *The Psychology of Hardy's Novels*. Queensland, Australia: University of Queensland Press, 1975.

Tomlinson, T. B. "Hardy's Universe: *Tess of the D'Urbervilles*." *The Critical Review* (Australia) 16 (1973): 19–38.

Waldoff, Leon. "Psychological Determinism in *Tess of the D'Urbervilles*." In *Critical Approaches to the Fiction of Thomas Hardy*, edited by Dale Kramer, 135–54. London: Macmillan, 1979.

Webster, Harvey Curtis. *On a Darkling Plain: The Art and Thought of Thomas Hardy*. Chicago: The University of Chicago Press, 1947.

Wing, George. "Tess and the Romantic Milkmaid." *Review of English Literature* 3 (1962): 22–30.

Woolf, Virginia. "Novels of Thomas Hardy." In *The Second Common Reader*, 266–80. New York: Harcourt, Brace, 1932.

———. "Half of Thomas Hardy." In *The Captain's Death Bed and Other Essays*, 62–68. New York: Harcourt, Brace, 1950.

Wright, Terence. "Rhetoric and Lyrical Imagery in *Tess of the D'Urbervilles*." *Durham University Journal* 34 (1973): 79–85.

Zabel, Morton Dauwen. "Hardy in Defense of His Art: The Aesthetic of Incongruity." *The Southern Review* 6 (1940–41): 125–49.

Acknowledgments

"Colour and Movement in Hardy's *Tess of the D'Urbervilles*" by Tony Tanner from *Critical Quarterly* 10, no. 3 (Autumn 1968), © 1968 by Tony Tanner. Reprinted by permission of the author.

" 'The Perfection of Species' and Hardy's Tess" by Bruce Johnson from *Nature and the Victorian Imagination*, edited by U. C. Knoepflmacher and G. B. Tennyson, © 1977 by The Regents of the University of California. Reprinted by permission of the University of California Press.

"Tess: The Making of a Pure Woman" by Mary Jacobus from *Tearing the Veil: Essays on Femininity*, edited by Susan Lipshitz, © 1978 by Routledge & Kegan Paul Ltd. Reprinted by permission. A version of this essay originally appeared in *Essays in Criticism* 26 (October 1976).

"*Tess of the D'Urbervilles*: Repetition as Immanent Design" by J. Hillis Miller from *Fiction and Repetition: Seven English Novels* by J. Hillis Miller, © 1982 by J. Hillis Miller. Reprinted by permission of the author, Harvard University Press, and Basil Blackwell Publishers.

"Pure Tess: Hardy on Knowing a Woman" by Kathleen Blake from *Studies in English Literature, 1500–1900* 22 (1982), © 1981 by William Marsh Rice University. Reprinted by permission.

"Hardy: 'Full-Hearted Evensong' " by Philip M. Weinstein from *The Semantics of Desire: Changing Models of Identity from Dickens to Joyce* by Philip M. Weinstein, © 1984 by Princeton University Press. Reprinted by permission of Princeton University Press.

Index

Analytical philosophy as interpretive
model, 76
Ancestry, 26–27, 29–30, 34, 36, 50,
66, 75
Aristophanes, 76–77
Arnold, Edward, 48
Arnold, Matthew, 36
Art and idealization, 99–100
Artistic form and interpretation, 83–85
Ascham, Roger, 51

Bagehot, Walter, 89–90
Baptism scene, 96–97
Bathsheba Everdene (*Far from the
Madding Crowd*), 98
Bayley, John, 100
"Beauty, The," 96
Beyond the Pleasure Principle (Freud), 77
Bible, the, 4, 74–75
Blackmoor Vale, 72, 92
Boldwood (*Far from the Madding Crowd*),
96
Bridehead, Sue (*Jude the Obscure*), 98
Brooks, Jean, 100–101

"Candour in English Fiction," 46, 48, 58,
60
Cause and effect in repetition, 72
Censorship: and critics, 45, 48, 49, 60;
Hardy's view of, 46–47, 49; and
purity, 45–49
Cerealia (May Festival), 25, 27, 31, 77,
91

Chase, the, 4, 54, 72, 92; as primeval
territory, 27; and sleep metaphor,
106
Christianity, 27; and capacity for
creating guilt, 28; impotence of,
74–75; interference of, 30; lost
innocence of, 34; traditional
morality of, 36–37, 46
Clare, Angel, 4, 9, 11, 18, 19, 54, 65, 66,
67, 68, 72, 85; as cause of Tess's
death, 12, 40–41; critics on, 49; and
first encounter with Tess, 78; and
generalization, 94; growth of, 46;
heterodoxy of, 55, 56–57; idealizing Tess, 48, 84, 88, 94, 96; and
Jocelyn Pierston, 99; married to
Tess, 10; moral principles vs.
emotion in, 108–9; "naturalism"
of, 36, 40, 42; and "newness," 33–
34, 40; as partner of Tess, 77–78;
psychology of, 31–32; purist point
of view of, 89, 108–9; and rejection of Tess, 14; religious disaffection of, 31, 55; reflectiveness of,
55; and reunion with Tess, 80;
revisions of, 51, 55–58; significance of name of, 74; sleepwalking
of, 12; on women, 10, 34–35, 48,
57, 81, 89–90, 95
Club-walking, 25–26, 52, 91, 92
Color and motion, 9–23. *See also* Landscape metaphor; Red imagery; Sun
imagery
Comma, use of, 82

Community: and home, 19; rejection of, 12

Consciousness: primitive, 94; and sleep, 105, 106

Cross-in-Hand, 14

Culture, types of, 37

Daniel Deronda (Eliot), 105

Darch, Car, 90, 113–14

Darwin, Charles, 41; on connectedness of all species, 42; Hardy's reaction to, 38–39; influence of, on Hardy, 27, 28, 35; perfection of species, 42–43

Darwin and Modern Science (Frazer), 42

Death, 11–12, 21, 63; as completeness, 79; and consciousness, 105; and desire for primal unity, 77, 80; and innocence, 80; and marriage, 12; as repose, 105; and separation, 13–14

DeLaura, David J., 36–37

Deracination and ancestry, 19, 34

Description, indirect, 81

Design and repetition, 65, 66, 72, 81. *See also* Repetition

Determinism and repetition, 79, 80–81

Difference, concept of, 61, 71

Disfigurement, 111, 112, 113, 114

"Dorsetshire Labourer, The," 93

Drabble, Margaret, 112

Druidical culture, 27

D'Urberville, Alec, 18, 75, 79, 81; attitude toward female sexuality, 48, 88; as cause of Tess's death, 12; conversion, 58–59; as false d'Urberville, 76; as manifestation of modern society, 19, 40; power of, 52; murder of, 14, 15, 39, 63, 68, 72; original version of, 51–52, 53; satanic qualities, 95

D'Urberville family: disappearance of, 20; evolution of, 38; and fatalism, 92–93; and grafting image, 65–66; and history, 91; melodramatic aspect of, 35; naturalness of, 36–

37, 38; passivity of, 92–93; violence of, 72, 93

Durbeyfield, Tess, 9, 41, 68; ancestry of, 26–27, 29–30, 50, 66, 75; and animal imagery, 91; compared to Angel Clare, 54–55; and compassion for animals, 42; as composite of stages, 26–27; cultural identity of, 115; death of, 11, 12, 80; divided self of, 13–14, 19, 115; Druidical past of, 27, 28; as a d'Urberville, 37–38; and d'Urbervilles, 36–37; as essence and type, 94; explanations of, 81–82; faith, 74–75; fierceness of, 35–36, 42; geographical movements of, 77; growth of, 50–51, 54–55; and history, 26, 65; individuality of, 50; innocence of, 28, 31; journey of, 66; and landscapes, 30–31; and legends, 72, 73; marriage of, 10, 12, 64; and murder of Alec, 14, 15, 39, 72; as natural, 28–30, 36–37, 73–74; nature vs. human in, 104–5, 108, 115; nature vs. society in, 19–20, 74; need for home, 18–19, 28; and oneness with all life, 42; as pagan, 11–12, 28, 29–30, 37, 41; potential of, 31; as pre-conscious physical presence, 107; purity of, 45, 87, 89, 90; recovery of, 29–30; and refusal to be stereotyped, 34, 95; and repetition, 70–72, 82–83; revisions of, 52–53, 58; sexuality of, 46, 49, 107, 112–13; suffering of, 59, 64, 75; transcendent sensibility of, 33; unbalance of, 59–60; and Ur-Tess, 47–48, 50, 52, 53, 57; as victim of men, 72; as victim of modern society, 41; violation of, 20, 54, 61–63, 106

Durbeyfield family, 27. *See also* Tess Durbeyfield

Dynasts, The, 1, 39, 99

Education vs. experience, 51

Egdon Heath (*The Return of the Native*),
27
"Ego and the Id, The" (Freud), 110
Eliot, George, 104
Ellis, Havelock, 45, 46
Emminster Vicarage, 14
Epipsychidion (Shelley), 2
Evolution: and altruism, 39; and con-
nectedness of all life forms, 38–39;
and consciousness, 37–38; Hardy's
viewpoint on, 38
Experience: and assimilation, 114–15;
vs. education, 51

Far from the Madding Crowd, 96, 98
Fate and repetition, 79, 80–81
Fawley, Jude (*Jude the Obscure*), 3, 4
Fertility as metaphor, 9–10, 25–26,
66–67
Flintcomb-Ash, 15, 18, 20, 50, 52, 58, 59,
77, 92
Folk culture, 37–38, 40
Folklore and Tess's history, 93
Frazer, James, 25, 28, 38, 39
Freud, Sigmund, 1, 6, 77, 78, 80, 110

Generalization: and Angel, 94; vs. indi-
viduality, 101–2
Geological metaphors, 25–26, 37; and
ancestry, 27; and paleontological
metaphors, 30; Victorian aware-
ness of, 38
God, absence of, 75
Golden Bough, The (Frazer), 25
Gose, Elliott B., 38–39
Grafting image, 66
Graphic, The, 63
Gregor, Ian, 106
Guest, Stephen (*The Mill on the Floss*),
105

Hardy, Florence Emily, 99
"Hardy and the Natural World"
(Drabble), 112
Hardy, Thomas: on altruism, 38–39;
attitude toward religion, 31;

biblical context of writing, 4–5;
on censorship, 46–47; censorship
of, 63; on character, 50–51;
compared to Angel Clare, 98–99;
criticism of, 48, 71, 100–101;
Darwin's influence on, 38–39, 43;
on death, 21; as devotee of the
ideal, 99–100; on evolution, 38; on
fate, 80–81; and generalization,
96–98; on Hodge, 93; and
Matthew Arnold, 36; on nature,
27–28, 33, 113; and perception,
93–94; and philosophers of understanding, 87; on prefaces, 69; and
preoccupation with movement, 14;
on purity, 45, 88; on repetition,
85–86; and sense of life, 21; and
sensitivity to language, 97–98;
Shelley's influence on, 89–90; on
social tradition, 83–84; on Stonehenge, 17–18; subversiveness of,
83–84; and Tess, 3–4, 45, 64, 69,
97; on theories of the universe, 21;
as tragic writer, 2, 20; vision of,
22; on women, 96–98. Works:
"Candour in English Fiction," 48,
58, 60; *The Dynasts*, 1, 39, 99; *Far
from the Madding Crowd*, 96, 98;
General Preface, 21; *Jude the
Obscure*, 3, 37, 45, 98; *A Laodicean*,
96; "The Profitable Reading of
Fiction," 98; *The Rainbow*, 22–23;
The Return of the Native, 3, 15–17,
21, 27; *The Tree of Knowledge*, 48;
The Woodlanders, 18. *See also Tess of
the D'Urbervilles*
Hawnferne, Mr., 51–52, 53, 54
Heath, 11, 16–17, 18, 21–22
Heliolatry. *See* Sun imagery
Hero vs. heroine, 95
Heterogeneity of literature, 71
History: of the D'Urbervilles, 38, 91;
inevitability of, 65
Hodge, 93, 94, 98
Home: and motion, 18; and transience,
14
Howe, Irving, 100

Hughes, Ted, 41
Humanity: career of, 104; and evolutionary oneness, 42–43; mobility of, 16–17; vs. nature, 17, 116; obliteration of, 17–18; and survival, 39–40; and will, 27–28
Hume, David, 87
Hyman, Stanley Edgar, 41–42

Immaculateness: and divided self, 115–16; vs. immersion, 110
Immanent design and repetition. *See* Repetition
Immanent will, 70, 79; personification of, 73; and sun imagery, 68
Impressions, use of, 77–78, 84
Impurity, 79. *See also* Purity
Individuality: vs. generalization, 95–96, 101–2; loss of, 94; and will, 106
Innocence and guilt in nature, 28
Interpenetration: and fulfillment, 116–17; and pulsation, 110; and values, 104–5, 108
Interpretations of *Tess*, 84–85
Intoxication motif, 54
"Intra Sepulchrum," 96
Ironical Tishbite, 5, 6, 74–75
Irony, 20–21, 28, 30; of life, 48; and reversal, 72

Joan, 26
John (Jack Durbeyfield), 25, 26, 50
Johnson, Lionel, 6–7, 103–4
Jude the Obscure, 3, 37, 45, 98

Kant, Immanuel, 87
Kettle, Arnold, 100
Knowledge: and dialectic of good and evil, 87; and subjectivity, 93–94; of women, 101–2

Laing, R. D., 115
Laird, J. T., 89
Landscape metaphor: and decaying architecture, 18; and history, 30–31, 37, 38; and human presence, 16–18; and journeying, 77; and marginlessness, 92, 96; and villages, 92
Lang, Andrew, 69, 115–16
Language, limits of, 97–98
Laodicean, A, 96
Lawrence, D. H., 2–3, 22–23, 89; and interpenetration, 104
Life: ephemeral nature of, 21; incompleteness of, 79; incomprehensibility of, 21; and motion, 18, 21–22
Linear sequentiality in Tess's life, 72
Literary criticism, on concept of woman, 100–101
Literature, heterogeneity of, 71
Lodge, David, 35–36
Love: and art, 99–100; and diffusion of personality, 91; and idealization, 99–100; and incompleteness, 99; and lovers' consciousness, 2
Lucas, John, 101

Machinery, image of, 18
Male–female relationships and primal unity, 77–78
Marginlessness, 98–99; and consciousness, 29; and personality, 90–93. *See also* Landscape metaphor
Marlott, 50, 54, 77
Marlott club-walking, 25–26, 52, 91, 92
Marriage and death, 12
May ceremony, 25, 27, 31, 77, 91
Measure, concept of, 75–76
Memory and repetition, 78
Metaphors: geological, 25–26, 27, 30, 37, 38; indirect, 62–63, 64
Miles, Rosalind, 101
"Milkmaid, The," 95–96
Miller, J. Hillis, 2, 4, 6, 89
Modernism, spirit of, 51
Moers, Ellen, 100
Morality: Christian, 36–38, 46; and impulse, 108–9; of retribution, 75
Morris, Mowbray, 48–49, 60

Motifs, mutually defining, 70
Motion, 27–28; and color, 15; inevitability of, 14; life and confusion, 18; sexual, 12; and struggle, 14–15. *See also* Landscape metaphor
Mythic patterning, 91
Mythology: comparative, 26; May ceremony, 25, 27, 31, 72, 91. *See also* Paganism; Red imagery; Sun imagery

Nature: cults, 91; deceptiveness of, 32–33; denial of, 13; and d'Urberville history, 38; and human behavior, 74; vs. humanity, 114–15, 116; indifference of, 112–13; innocence and guilt in, 28; interpenetration of human world, 104–5, 108; and loss of personality, 112; man's inhumanity toward, 73–74; and marginlessness, 90–91; as objectionable, 32–33; power of duplication, 91; and purity, 88; as self-sufficient entity, 29; and sexuality, 91, 113; vs. society, 19–20, 74; and Tess's inheritance, 32; vs. law, 19–20
Newness, 33–34, 40
Nineteenth-century sensibility, 37
Novels: center of, 81; mobility as central theme in, 16–17; radical structure of, 17

Old Testament, 74–75
Oliphant, Mrs., 46, 50, 53, 59
Omens, 9–10
Original unity, concept of, 76–77
Origin of Species (Darwin), 27

Paganism: and consciousness, 27; and fertility and sexuality rites, 25–26; and home, 28; and survival of the fittest, 41; and women, 11
Paradox and repetition, 65
Past: awareness of, 33; and present, 38. *See also* Ancestry

Paulin, Tom, 87
"Pedigree, The," 96
Perception and perceiver's mind, 93–94
Personality and marginlessness, 29, 90–93, 98–99
Pierston, Jocelyn (*The Well-Beloved*), 89, 99
Plato, 76
Power, Paula (*A Laodicean*), 96
Prefaces, 83–84; General, 21; repetition in, 68–69
President of the Immortals, 73
Primal unity, 77–78
Primitive Culture (Tylor), 39
Prince, death of, 18, 50, 52, 63, 79
"Profitable Reading of Fiction, The," 98
Pulse beat, metaphor of, 108, 110, 111
Purity, 79, 84; and censorship, 45–60; definitions of, 88–89; as erotic, 95; as generic, 90, 95; and nature, 88

Rainbow, The (Lawrence), 22–23
Reader: interpretation of *Tess*, 70–71; and question of repetition, 71–72
Reading as deciphering, 84, 85
Reality, general vs. particular, 88
Red imagery, 10, 11, 20, 21; and immanent will, 67–69; meaning of, 67–68
Redemptive theolatry, 36
Repetition, 4; and design, 65, 66, 72, 81; and fate, 79, 80–81; gaps and continuity in, 65; and history, 65; immanent, 83; and impression, 78–79; and marking, 65; and measure, 75–76; of natural behavior, 73–74; and novelist, 69; and prefaces, 68–69; purpose of, 64–65; question of, 61, 70, 71–72; temporal, 91; and writing, 65
Return of the Native, The, 3, 15–17, 21, 27

Sandbourne, 59, 77
Schoolmaster (Ascham), 51
Schopenhauer, Arthur, 1, 6, 27, 39
Setting and human situation, 105–6

Sexes, incompatibility of, 76–77
Sexuality, 63; and autonomy, 46; and
    death, 12; and disfigurement, 114;
    double standard of morality, 49–
    50; female, 48; and motion, 12;
    and nature, 91, 112–13; objectifi-
    cation of, 34; and personality, 91;
    rape vs. seduction, 106; and
    writing, 65, 69
Shelley, Percy Bysshe, 1, 4, 87, 89–90
Sign-painter as symbol, 54, 82
Sleep metaphor, 107–8; and conscious-
    ness, 105, 106; and emotional
    torment, 109–10
Slopes, the, 51, 54
Society: insecurity of, 73; limitations of,
    29, 36–37; modern, 19, 40; vs.
    nature, 74; power relationships in,
    83–84; as unnatural, 19–20
Sorrow, 47, 48, 51, 79
Spencer, Herbert, 39, 98
Stewart, J. I. M., 104
Stoke-d'Urbervilles, 66
Stonehenge, 41, 80; altar of, 11, 66;
    arrest scene at, 107–8; as human
    structure, 17–18; as pagan home,
    26, 28, 33
Structure, importance of, 17–18
Study of Thomas Hardy (Lawrence), 3
Subject, transformation of, 98–99
Sun imagery, 9–12, 20, 41, 85; ancestral
    worship of, 28; and consciousness,
    28; description of rays, 67; as fer-
    tility symbol, 9–10, 66–67; and
    immanent will, 68
Survival theme, 39–40
Symposium (Plato), 76–77

Taine, Hippolyte-Adolphe, 99
Talbothays, 11, 30, 77, 78, 91
Teleology in Hardy's works, 41
Tess of the D'Urbervilles, 3, 45, 61; analyti-
    cal interpretation of, 76–77;
    Biblical interpretation of, 74–75;
    Christian imagery in, 9, 59; color
    theme in, 9–23; connectedness of
    passages in, 69–71; crisis vs.

penetration in, 116–17; effect of,
    on Hardy, 64, 68; elemental
    system of, 70–72; as experiment in
    survival, 40; family tradition in,
    72–73; fatalistic interpretation of,
    80–81; geological metaphors in,
    25–43, 71; Hardy's definition of,
    83; interpretations of, 71–83; irony
    in, 20–21, 28, 30, 48, 72; judgment
    in, 20–21; motifs in, 70–72; nar-
    rator of, 85; naturalistic interpre-
    tation of, 73–74; and 1902 text, 59;
    omens in, 9, 10; permutation in,
    70–72; and post-1889 phase of
    composition, 58; prefaces to, 21,
    68–69, 83–84; and reader, 70–72;
    repetition in, 4, 6–7, 61–86, 91;
    revisions of, 47–48, 50–60, 89; as
    sequence of seasons, 71; sex-role
    stereotyping in, 95–98; subtitle of,
    68–69, 74, 84, 88; as tragedy of
    thwarted potential, 48; and truth
    to life, 58
"Tess's Lament," 63–64, 79, 80
Time: failure of, 79; and structure, 18
Tishbite (Elijah), 5, 6, 74–75
"Too Late, Beloved," 57, 79
Totemism (Frazer), 39
Transcendence, and good and evil, 104
Trantridge, 54, 59, 77, 90, 91
Tree of Knowledge, The (Hardy), 48
Troy, Sergeant (Far from the Madding
    Crowd), 98
Truth, 58, 70–71
Tulliver, Maggie (The Mill on the Floss),
    103, 105
Two Gentlemen of Verona (Shakespeare),
    64, 69
Tylor, Sir Edward Burnett, 27, 28, 38,
    39, 42

Ursula (The Rainbow), 22–23

Vale of Blackmoor, 72, 92
Vale of the Little Dairies, 92
Valley of the Great Dairies, 77
Values and human career, 104

Van Ghent, Dorothy, 100
Var Vale, 38
Vengeance theme, 75
Venn, Diggory (*The Return of the Native*), 21
Vertical vs. horizontal, 13
Villages, 92
Violence: biblical explanation of, 75; pattern of, 81; and sexuality, 114
Virginity theme, 104, 111
Vye, Eustacia, (*The Return of the Native*), 16, 17

"Wasted Illness, A," 13
Well-Beloved, The, 89, 90; and loss of individuality, 94; and loss of love, 99

Wildeve, Damon (*The Return of the Native*), 21, 22
Will, 39; immanent, 68, 70, 73, 79, 81; individual, 106
Women: as antisocial, 29; contiguousness of, 94; critics on, 100–101; double standard for, 48, 94–95; as generic, 88, 89–90, 91; Hardy on, 97; loss of personality of, 90; objectification of, 34, 89–90, 91; as pagan, 30; sex-role stereotyping of, 97–98; understanding of, 88
Woodlanders, The, 18
World as Will and Representation, The (Schopenhauer), 1
Writing: and sexuality, 69; and violence, 65